The Diary of Mary Elizabeth Auman Seagrove, North Carolina 1928–1930

◆

Proto-Feminist in the Age of Jazz

The Diary of Mary Elizabeth Auman Seagrove, North Carolina 1928–1930

◆

Proto-Feminist in the Age of Jazz

Transcribed and Edited by
William Thomas Auman

iUniverse, Inc.
New York   Bloomington

The Diary of Mary Elizabeth Auman, Seagrove, North Carolina, 1928–1930
Proto-Feminist in the Age of Jazz

iUniverse books may be ordered through booksellers or by contacting:

iUniverse
1663 Liberty Drive
Bloomington, IN 47403
www.iuniverse.com
1-800-Authors (1-800-288-4677)

Because of the dynamic nature of the Internet, any Web addresses or links contained in this book may have changed since publication and may no longer be valid.

ISBN: 978-1-4401-9944-8 (sc)
ISBN: 978-1-4401-9943-1 (dj)
ISBN: 978-1-4401-9942-4 (ebk)

Printed in the United States of America

iUniverse rev. date: 7/26/2010

Dedication

To the memory of the members of the first class to graduate from Seagrove
High School—the class of 1928:

Mary Auman
Vada Graves
Maple Lawrence
Lane Russell
Alberta Auman
Bill Matthews
Vernitia Stutts
Howard Auman
Harwood Graves
Elijah Lucas
Alta Matthews
Fred Auman
Walter Macon
Martha Graves

Contents

Preface

On a clear autumn afternoon in the late 1950s, I returned home after a trying day as a student at Asheboro High School. I found my father in his office cleaning out his safe. I noticed a large packet of yellowed papers he had set aside to discard. They were mostly old deeds pertaining to land he had purchased over the years. The oldest deed was dated 1787. I have an instinctive affection for things old, so I asked him if I could have them. I could not bear to see them destroyed. He not only gave me the deeds, he gave me some old letters, business papers, photographs, and a diary. The diary belonged to his sister, my Aunt Mary. The diary covered the years 1928 to 1930.

For more than two decades, I kept the papers my father gave me in storage as I moved around from place to place. In 1984, I was working on a doctorate in history at the University of North Carolina at Chapel Hill. As a graduate student, I secured a part-time job on campus at the Southern Historical Collection processing manuscript collections. It dawned on me that I had found the ideal place to deposit the old deeds, letters, photographs, diary, and other items I had been saving all these years. I asked my supervisor if I could establish a manuscript collection called the Auman Family Papers. He answered in the affirmative.

Graham Auman of Raleigh visited the Southern Historical Collection to view the Auman Family Papers. He alerted the curator that he had a grandmother who, when she died in 1969, left behind two trunks full of old papers. Among them were more than two thousand letters dating from the 1850s to the 1950s. In 2001, Graham Auman and Catherine Auman DeMaere of Chapel Hill donated these papers to the Auman Family Papers, which brought the total number of documents in the collection to more than seven thousand items.

About five years ago, I decided to publish Mary's diary. Unfortunately, Mary did not take the time to make thoughtful entries that revealed her innermost feelings. Quite the contrary, she hurriedly jotted down brief observations of the day's events. Nevertheless, Mary's pithy comments about the people and events swirling around her offer valuable insights into the everyday life of a middle-class teenage girl living in the rural south of the late 1920s. Numerous photographs in the published diary furnish additional important information about the world that Mary lived in.

Since Mary hastily made entries in her diary with no thought that anyone would likely read them, I have decided to add periods where they were left out, capitalize first words in sentences when not done, correct misspelled words, and rectify most errors in grammar. I add words or comments in brackets when needed to clarify what Mary is writing. I have tried to identify every person, subject, and place mentioned in the diary; when I do not do so, that means that I was unable to make an identification. I decided not to identify the composers of popular songs mentioned in the diary.

Acknowledgments

I would like to thank the Southern Historical Collection, Wilson Library, University of North Carolina at Chapel Hill, for allowing me to publish the "Mary Elizabeth Auman Diary, 1928 to 1930." The diary is part of collection number 4401, the Auman Family Papers. I am also grateful to them for granting me permission to publish twenty-four photographs from the Auman Family Papers.

I owe a special debt to Katie Nash, Special Collections Librarian and Archivist at the Belk Library, Elon University, for providing me with guidance and assistance in using the university archives and for making me copies of photographs in the university yearbook. I would also like to thank the Elon University Archives and Special Collection Department of Belk Library for permission to reproduce images from the *Phi Psi Cli* Yearbook collection. Thanks go out to Marsha Haithcock and the staff at the Randolph Room, Asheboro Public Library, for providing me with copies of photographs and assistance in using microfilms. I am grateful to Elise Allison, assistant archivist at the Greensboro Historical Museum, Archives Division, for providing me with copies of photographs of downtown Greensboro during the 1920s and '30s, and to the staff at the May Memorial Library, Burlington, North Carolina, for copies of photographs of downtown Burlington in the 1930s.

I would like to thank Clem Paffe of Asheboro for rehabilitating several damaged and faded old photographs used in this diary. Clem was also kind enough to make several photographs for me. In addition, I thank the following people for providing me with photographs: Dorothy and Walter Auman, Paul Lucas, Nancy Auman Cunningham, Frank Sprague, Auman Teel, and Beulah Luck.

Chapter 1

Auman Family History

Image 2: Frank Auman home at Auman's Crossroads, about 1910, where Mary was born. Alpheus Auman on roof, Frank on porch.

Mary Elizabeth Auman was born on April 17, 1912, at Auman's Crossroads, a rural farm community located in Union township in south-central Randolph County, North Carolina. She was a descendant of German immigrants who arrived in Philadelphia in 1730 and lived in Pennsylvania and Maryland for three generations before moving to North Carolina in 1791.[1] Her father, Frank Auman (1883–1941), was a farmer and a businessman. Frank was a son of farmers Franklin (1826–1911) and Elizabeth (née Ward, 1842–1892) Auman. Between 1903 and 1905, he attended Trinity Park High School in Durham and Guilford College near Greensboro.[2] He taught for at least one term at the Mountain School, a Randolph County one-room public school located about one mile north of Auman's Crossroads. Before he married in 1909, Frank had gained business experience by clerking at a general merchandise store in Star and operating a small general store in Ulah. Mary's mother was Mattie Auman (1888–1963), daughter of Charlie T. (1861–1932) and Mary E. (née Allred, 1860–1912) Luck of the White House community

1

that was located about five miles northwest of Auman's Crossroads. She was a 1908 graduate of Why Not Academy, a private secondary and public elementary school situated about one mile southeast of Seagrove, a village about four miles to the east of Auman's Crossroads. Mary had an older brother, Howard (1911–1998), and a younger sister, Mabel (1914–1968).[3]

In 1896, the Asheboro and Aberdeen Railway Company built a railroad between Asheboro and the Montgomery County line that ran southward to Aberdeen and Troy. About twelve miles south of Asheboro, the railroad company built a depot that they named Seagroves in honor of one of their civil engineers. Seagrove—the painter dropped the final "s" in "Seagroves" when he ran out of space on the station sign—soon began to grow as land speculators and businesses moved into the community. By 1930, the population of Seagrove totaled 245 persons. The rural road that ran south from Asheboro to Carthage and Troy, the seats of Moore and Montgomery counties respectively, was often impassable during inclement weather. In 1912, a group of one hundred and twelve entrepreneurs in Asheboro and southern Randolph County pledged over four thousand dollars to finance the construction of an all-weather gravel highway complete with side-ditches that ran from Asheboro to the Moore County line. This new highway passed through the center of Seagrove. (In 1927, the state paved this road and designated it a part of U.S. Route 220.)[4]

Image 3: Frank Auman at work on his farm at Auman's Crossroads, about 1910.

Enticed by the developing economic opportunities, Frank Auman bought a lot on Main Street situated about two hundred feet east of the Seagrove depot. He moved his family into a new house that he built there in 1913.[5] Over the next few years, he owned a sawmilling business, speculated in real estate, became part owner in a hardware store, invested in a bank, served as United States postmaster at Seagrove (1914–20), and owned and operated a general store. However, it was in the lumber business that he made his mark. By the late 1920s, his Seagrove Lumber Company, a business that he bought in 1926 from Arthur Ross of Asheboro, was becoming one of the leading lumber companies in the central part of the state.[6]

A house and lot belonging to David A. Cornelison (1876–1964) adjoined Frank Auman's property to the west. Dave was married to Belle Luck (1886–1968), Frank's sister-in-law. He owned and operated a dry-goods store located next to his house. Mary was very close to her Aunt Belle and Uncle Dave. In her diary, she records frequent visits to their home and store. In the winter of 1913, the citizens of Seagrove selected Frank Auman and Dave Cornelison to go to Raleigh to petition the state legislature to incorporate the town, which it did on March 5. Dave Cornelison became Seagrove's first mayor and Frank Auman one of the first town commissioners.[7]

Mary's uncle, Ivey Burch Luck (1897–1989), a brother of Mattie Auman and Belle Cornelison, attended the Farm Life School in Moore County after he completed his elementary education. Farm Life was a secondary boarding school where students could earn part of their tuition, room, and board by working on the school farm. Sometime after he left there, he moved to Seagrove to seek his fortune. He boarded with the Cornelisons while he worked at various jobs, including clerking at the Cornelisons' dry-goods store and working at the Seagrove Lumber Company.[8] He soon purchased land on the east end of Main Street just past the Frank Auman residence where he built and operated a combination service station, grocery store, and café. Mary frequently mentions Ivey in her diary.

Lebbeus Auman (1885–1949), Frank's brother and Mary's uncle, attended a private military school for his secondary education.[9] He served in the U.S. Army as a noncommissioned officer for about thirty years. The Army assigned Lebbeus to the Panama Canal Zone for his first tour of duty; he served the remainder of his military career at Fort Eustis and Langley Field, Virginia. He married Bertha Mae Luck (1890–1970), a daughter of Charlie and Mary Luck. (Note that the brothers Frank and Lebbeus Auman married the sisters Mattie and Bertha Luck.) Lebbeus and Bertha Auman had three children: twin sons Samuel and Thomas, and daughter, Evelyn. Mary refers to her Uncle "Leb," Aunt Bertha, and their children at various times in her diary.

Image 4: Cadet Lebbeus Auman (right), about 1902,
student at a private military academy.

Chapter 2

Seagrove High School Days

Mary attended the Seagrove public schools. In 1920, the county built a new schoolhouse a few yards to the east of her home. It provided both elementary and secondary levels of instruction. Due to overcrowding, the county constructed a new nine-room brick schoolhouse in 1926 about one-quarter mile northeast of the Frank Auman residence. Instruction included elementary grades one through seven and high school grades eight through eleven.[10]

Mary's diary opens in January 1928, when she was a senior at Seagrove High School. She and her brother Howard were members of the first class to graduate from Seagrove High School—the class of 1928. She writes about her academic studies, her teachers, and her school social life. She records the coming of electricity and the radio to Seagrove and the arrival of talking pictures to movie theaters. Mary often refers to the 1928 presidential election between democrat Al Smith and republican Herbert Hoover; she was an Al Smith supporter. Mary takes many trips to High Point, Greensboro, and Asheboro, where she shops and attends movies. She has many friends in Asheboro, the seat of Randolph County, where she frequently goes to parties, to movies, and on dates. Mary also comments on the many trips that she takes to visit friends and relatives in other communities and towns.

Image 5: Dave and Belle Cornelison, about 1908.

The Diary

January 1928

January 1
To-day, being very cold, I spent the better part of it at home reading "David Copperfield." [*David Copperfield* is a novel written by Charles Dickens.]

January 2
Returned to school to-day after Christmas vacation and received my Geometry mid-term exam paper, which was perfect. [There were six teachers at Seagrove School: Harvey White of Greensboro, the principal; Charlie and Lillie O'Quinn of Star; Verda Morgan and Thryra Wright of Asheboro; and Marie Wrenn of Franklinville. White and the O'Quinns taught high-school classes. The O'Quinns were siblings or otherwise related.[11]]

January 3
Attended school today and visited new laboratory in the north-west room.

January 4
Attended school today. Returned home and wrote a composition on "the Life of Julius Caesar."

Image 6: Frank and Mattie Auman house, Seagrove, North Carolina, about 1920 (house built in 1913).

January 5
Mabel's birthday—14 yrs. old. Vada and I came thru the pasture to town from school. Then home. [Mabel Auman (1914–68) was Mary's sister. Vada Graves was a close friend who lived on the north side of Seagrove about one quarter of a mile from the Mary Auman residence. She would be Mary's roommate at Elon College in the fall. Vada was the daughter of Hiram and Stella Graves. According to the census, Hiram's occupation in 1930 was truck driver.[12]]

January 6
Took final exam on Caesar this morning (made 98) afternoon! Seagrove played scheduled basket ball game with Bennett. Score 18–15 in favor of Seag. V. & I ransacked dinner baskets. [Mary did not make clear whether she meant "morning" or "afternoon." Bennett is a hamlet located in southwestern Chatham County.]

Image 7: Seagrove High School basketball team, 1927–28: (*standing, left to right*)
Thurman Cox, James Comer, Lane Russell; (*squatting, left to right*)
Howard Auman, Leslie Auman.

January 7 Saturday
Rode Howard's new horse to the dam and spring in our pasture this morning. This evening read Shakespeare's "Othello." [Howard Auman (1911–98) was Mary's brother.]

January 8
Went to Sunday school this morning. This afternoon: visited Uncle David and Aunt Belle. This evening: went to church. [Belle Cornelison (née Luck) was a sister of Mary's mother, Mattie.]

January 9
Attended school today. Read "Lorna Doane." [*Lorna Doone* is a novel written by Richard Blackmore.]

January 10
Attended school today and spent the afternoon in the library with Raeford Williams, who with Howard in a car wreck got his leg broke. [As Howard drove south out of Asheboro in foggy weather, he slammed into the rear of a truck ahead of him, injuring Raeford Williams, a passenger in his car. Raeford, age about eighteen, was the son of Wister and Cannie Williams, farmers living in Union Township several miles west of Seagrove.[13]]

January 11
Spent the afternoon in the library reporting on Shakespeare's "Midsummer Night's Dream" with Vada & Martha Graves, Louis Tucker, Harwood Graves & Leslie Auman. [Martha and Harwood Graves and their siblings, Philmore and Della Mae Graves, ages about seventeen, eighteen, twenty-three, and thirteen respectively, were the children of Delphia and Della Graves, farmers who lived in the Why Not community. Leslie Wade Auman (1908–72) was a son of Pearson and Jennie Auman, farmers who lived in Union Township. Leslie was a member of the Seagrove High School basketball team during the 1927–28 basketball season. In September 1929, Leslie Auman enrolled as a freshman at the University of North Carolina at Chapel Hill.[14]]

January 12
Tried our first experiment in the laboratory to-day, which was constructing & using the hygrometer. Mr. White forbids the senior class studying in the library together because we "sang" too much. [Harvey E. White, high school teacher and principal of Seagrove School, roomed at the Eli Leach household in Seagrove. A hygrometer is an instrument used to measure humidity.[15]]

January 13

The "Athenian Literary Society" entertained the "parent-teachers association" tonight. I spent this afternoon in the Music room studying & practicing a piano solo, which I played tonight. S.H.S. basketball team played Star. Heard two heavyweights, Sharkey & Heeney fight to-night over radio. [Star is a small town located about eight miles south of Seagrove in Montgomery County. The Tom Heeney–Jack Sharkey fight was a draw; Sharkey lost to Gene Tunney in July 1928 in a contest for the world heavyweight title.[16]]

January 14 Saturday

Vada spent last night with me. Visited my great aunt, Mrs. H.D. Smith this afternoon. Howard is seventeen to-day. [Mrs. H.D. Smith was the wife of H. Duckery Smith, janitor at the Seagrove School. They lived in northwest Seagrove near Vada Graves.[17]]

Image 8: Mary's grandfather, Charlie T. Luck (1861–1932), around 1920.

January 15

Went to my grandfather's this morning. Rudolph & Anna Grace Frazier & Bonnie Davis were there. After lunch, we went to the "Cat Fish Hole." The scenery was very beautiful. Rudolph especially thought so. [Charles "Charlie" T. Luck (1861–1932) was Mary's maternal grandfather. He lived on a farm located about seven miles northwest of Seagrove in Cedar Grove Township. Charlie was a farmer and a deputy sheriff. The Cat Fish Hole was a natural swimming pool in the Little River, a stream that ran through the Luck property.]

January 16
I began new week in school this morning. Had mid-term exam on history (United States). Bill Boroughs came to see Howard. Bill has just come home from Port Arthur, Texas, & Mobile ala [Alabama].

January 17
Martha [Graves] spent last night with me. We studied for geography exam which we had today.

January 18
Exams. being over, I had a good time at school to-day playing ball and bicycle racing. Read O. Henry's "Cabbage and Rings" tonight. ["Honor Roll" students in the senior class at Seagrove High School—those who made a grade of "B" or better for the fourth month of the school year—were Mary Auman, Howard

Image 9: Frank and Mattie Auman, Seagrove, North Carolina, about 1924.

Auman, Elijah Lucas, Vada Graves, Martha Graves, and Lane Russell. One student—Alta Mae Matthews—made As on all subjects.[18]]

January 19
Read "the Oregon Trail" today. [*The Oregon Trail* is a novel by Francis Parkman.]

January 20
Went to Bennett to-day to see the ball game between Seagrove and Bennett. The latter won by score of 39–11.

January 21 Saturday
Embroidered a tea apron this afternoon. Heard that Billy Hughes is very sick. Seagrove H.S. boys gave Negro minstrel [show] here to-night. [Not able to locate a witness to this show, the editor presumes that the boys performed it in blackface. Students staged a second "Negro minstrel show" at Seagrove School on November 10 of this year. Billy Hughes—a son of Mamie Hughes—was Mary's first cousin. Mamie was a daughter of Charlie and Mary Luck.]

January 22
Went to Sunday school this morning. Alberta Auman visited me this afternoon and we made candy and parched corn. To-night Edith Brower & Edith McDowell visited me from Asheboro. [Edith Brower was a daughter of Curtis Brower, a lumber dealer; Edith McDowell was a daughter of Joseph McDowell, a chauffeur; they both lived on Walker Avenue in south Asheboro. Alberta Auman (1910–2001) was a daughter of Artemus R. (1872–1942) and Lora (née Yow, 1880–1973) Auman, owners of Seagrove Hardware.[19]]

January 23
Mr. Hicks, from Asheboro, had a wreck this morning when he ran into Boode Bean's truck. The car turned over in our yard. [Boodie Horatio Bean (1905–89), age about twenty-two at this time, was a son of Horatio L. and Adline Bean, farmers living in Union Township west of Seagrove. Boodie, then employed at Frank Auman's Seagrove Lumber Company as a truck driver, was a close friend of the Auman family. In the 1920 Federal Census, the name is spelled "Brodie." In the *North Carolina Death Collection,* it is spelled "Boodie."[20]]

January 24
Electric lights are now beginning to be installed in Seagrove. This afternoon the post was erected in front of our house.

Image 10: Seagrove School, around 1928

January 25
Today, during Geography period, we looked at pictures of many points of interest in all parts of the world.

January 26
Our class planned to go to Caraway Mountains this afternoon but Mr. White detained us. [The Caraway Mountains are located about three miles northwest of Asheboro. They are a subset of the Uwharrie Mountains, the oldest mountain range in North America.]

January 27
Read O. Henry's "Four Million" to-day.

January 28 Saturday
Snowed last night. Mabel and I skated this morning. Obsira Leach visited me this afternoon. [Oberia Leach, age about twelve, was the daughter of Garet and Grace Leach. The Leaches lived in Seagrove near the school; Garet was an auto mechanic.[21]]

January 29
Went to Sunday school this morning. Visited Alberta Auman this afternoon. Attended C.E. tonight. [Christian Endeavor (C.E.) was an interdenominational, international Christian social group. It originated at a church in Maine in 1881, and by 1899, it had over 3.5 million members worldwide. Membership was strongest among Baptists, Methodists, and Presbyterians.[22]]

Image 11: Dave Cornelison's dry-goods store, Seagrove,
North Carolina, around 1940.

January 30
Went to Uncle David's store last night and heard President Coolidge and
vicepresident [Charles Gates Dawes] speak over radio.

January 31
Read "Oliver Twist" today. [A novel by Charles Dickens.]

February 1928

February 1
Attended C.E. Social at Maple Lawrence's home to-night. Was accompanied home by W.E. Tyler. [The Christian Endeavor meeting lasted from 7:30 to 10:00 PM. It opened with a business session followed by contests, games, and refreshments. About thirty people attended. Maple Lawrence (b. 1909) was a daughter of Oscar and Ida Lawrence, farmers. She, along with Mary, was a freshman at Elon College in the fall of 1928.[23]]

February 2
Went to Uncle David's store tonight and heard radio.

February 3
Hemp played basketball game with Seagrove today. Score was 24–22 in Seagrove's favor. Went to Star tonight and heard "Mammy's Lil' Wild Rose"— Senior Play. [*The Courier*, a newspaper issued weekly from Asheboro, reported that the contestants played hard from the beginning of the game to the end. Howard Auman "starred" for Seagrove, and a player named Brown led the Hemp team. According to *The Courier*, the final score was 24 to 21.[24]]

Image 12: "The Big Four," Seagrove High's BMOC (Big Men On Campus) in 1928: (*left to right*) Elijah Lucas, Fred Auman, Howard Auman, Harwood Graves. In the fall, all of them would enroll at the University of North Carolina.

February 4 Saturday
Alberta, Norma, Ruby, and I went to Uncle David's store to-night to hear radio. Had much fun learning to make "crows feet" and "Jacobs Ladder." [Perhaps "crows feet" and "Jacob's Ladder" were patterns cut out of folded paper.]

February 5
Nina Beane went with us to Grandpa's today. Ruby Brooks and Norma Brown visited me to-night & as it rained, we could not have C.E. so Miss O'Quinn, Tyler & myself heard radio. [Miss O'Quinn was a teacher at Seagrove School. Nina Bean, age about sixteen, was a sister of Boodie Bean. See entry for January 23, 1928, for information on the Bean family.]

February 6
Received our senior playbooks. Was very much surprised to find that I was to play the part of "Liza Stuebbin"—the village gossip.

February 7
Went to Hemp with Fred & Lane & Vada this afternoon to the basketball game between Seagrove and Elise. Score was 14–12 in the latter's favor. Saw Vera & Treva Lynch & Norva Beane. [Elsie was the name of the public school at Hemp.]

February 8
Went to a party to-night at the home of Mrs. John Sikes given for the "power line" boys. "Wake Forest" (Davis Perry) was my partner. Played "Wink." [John and Myrtle Sikes, ages about thirty-five and thirty-three respectively, were farmers living in the Seagrove community.[25]]

February 9
Had a hard time getting permission from Mr. & Miss. O'Quinn to watch Tyler & Newton work at the streetlight in front of the schoolhouse today. [Tyler and Newton were two of the "power line boys."]

February 10
Went to parent-teachers meeting at schoolhouse tonight. "Wake Forest" was there.

February 11 Saturday
Stayed with Alberta tonight. Leta took us to ride and we visited Romie Harman. [Leta and Alberta Auman were sisters.]

February 12
Attended church this afternoon and to-night.

February 13
Our house was wired [for electricity] to-day.

February 14
Miss Lena Russell gave a Valentine Party to-night in honor of the senior class. Miss Russell is our Geometry Tr. [teacher] Met *Tyler* in front of the café. His last night in *Seagrove*. [The Valentine party started at 7:30 PM. The attendees partook in games and contests. Howard Auman and Vada Graves won the contest "Cupid's Pets." The host served refreshments.[26]]

Image 13: Maude Lee Spoon's Music Class, Seagrove School, 1923, including Howard Auman, top left; Mabel Auman, second row, second from right; and Mary Auman, standing behind Mabel.

February 15
Stood State intelligence test this morning. Told Tyler good-by this afternoon at four o'clock.

February 16
Practiced play most of the day on stage.

February 17
The lights were first turned on in Seagrove this afternoon. Our Literary Society entertained the eighth grade this morning by giving a Lincoln Program. [The town of Seagrove now had twenty streetlights. One may find it curious to come across southerners presenting a "Lincoln Program" at a public school in the south in 1928. Perhaps one reason for this anomaly had to do with the fact that Randolph County and all the surrounding counties had a strong anti-Confederate, pro-Union element in its population during the Civil War. Many of them were outspoken supporters of Abraham Lincoln. [27]]

February 18 Saturday
To-day being bitter cold I spent the greater part of it at home. Seagrove played a ball game with Star to-night.

February 19
Received letter this morning from Tyler, who is now at Autreyville, North Carolina. The weather being very cold I stayed at home & read and played the piano.

February 20
Seagrove played a ball game with Asheboro to-day & was defeated.

February 21
Today we practiced senior play. I began reading "The Americanization of Edward Bok." [A Pulitzer Prize–winning autobiography of a noted publisher and editor.]

February 22
Finished the "Americanization of Edward Bok" to-day.

February 23
Seagrove H.S. played a ball game with Star this afternoon. Went to a party to-night given by Jim and Joseph Comer. [James R. "Jim" and Joseph "Joe" Comer, ages about eighteen and twenty-one respectively in 1928, were sons of James R. and Cora M. Comer, farmers living in Biscoe Township, Montgomery County, North Carolina, in 1920. Their sister, May S. Comer, age about twenty-one in 1920, was a public-school teacher living with her parents. Sometime before 1930, the Comers moved to Seagrove, where the census listed Mr. Comer's occupation as farmer.[28]]

February 24
Read "Henry Esmond" to-day. [A novel by William Makepeace Thackeray.]

February 25 Saturday
Louise, Susan, and Helen King visited me this afternoon. [Ages ten, six, and three respectively, they were the daughters of Elsie and Harriett King, farmers. The Kings resided across Main Street from the Aumans.[29]]

February 26
Went to my grandfather's to-day.

February 27
Practiced our Senior play to-night. First time the lights were turned on in school house.

February 28
Spent the morning in the library making posters and handbills to advertise our play.

February 29
Practiced play to-night. Had much fun teasing Martha [Graves] about being "READY." [Mary wrote the word "READY" in a bold Gothic-like script. In the parlance of the time and place, a person was "ready" when he or she was mature enough, physically and emotionally, to engage with a member of the opposite gender on an adult basis.]

March 1928

March 1
Miss Russell kept Martha in for chewing "chewing gum." One year ago to-night the "Big Snow" fell. [On the night of March 1, 1927, twenty-six inches of snow fell in Seagrove. See "Important Events" at end of diary.]

March 2
Decorated stage this afternoon for play. Lane, Vada, and I went down to Mr. Millers & got trailing cedar. Gave full dress rehearsal of play to-night.

March 3 Saturday
"THE ROMANCE HUNTERS" given by Seagrove High School Seniors tonight. Mr. O'Quinn director—

March 4
Went to Sunday school this morning. Visited Martha and Della Mae Graves this afternoon.

Image 14: General Store at Ulah, North Carolina, about 1910. Frank Auman standing in doorway, Charlie Luck sitting in buggy pulled by white horse.

March 5
Began reading "The Deerslayer" to-day. [A novel written by James Fennimore Cooper.]

March 6
Taught the fifth and sixth grades to-day in the absence of their teacher, Miss Verda Morgan. [Verda Morgan, age about twenty-two in 1928, came from the Tabernacle community of western Randolph County.[30]]

March 7
Received my subject for my 1000 word composition to-day. It was: "New York City as a Commercial Center."

March 8
Daddy got a new electric radio to-day.

March 9
The tenth grade entertained the Parent teachers to-night by presenting one of the Carolina Playmaker's Plays: "Peggy." [The Carolina Playmakers are based at the University of North Carolina at Chapel Hill.]

March 10 Saturday
Vada visited me this afternoon and we went to see Louise Smith, who is leaving to-morrow for Florida.

March 11
Attended church to-day. Mr. Cumming preached on: "The Second Coming of our Lord." [Reverend J.C. Cummings was a minister from Hemp.[31]]

March 12
Had test on literature, Book IV to-day.

March 13
Had test on Geography and History to-day. Mr. White, Miss O'Quinn, Mr. O'Quinn & Miss Wrenn visited us to-night. [These were all teachers at Seagrove School.]

March 14
The Seniors took the Juniors & teachers on a picnic and wiener roast to "Cotton Stone" mountain this afternoon. I went to Asheboro to the show to-night with Mr. White.

March 15
Vada & I helped Elijah Lucas drag the baseball ground this morning. [Elijah Lucas, age about twenty-one, was the son of Sylvester and Della Lucas, farmers. He was one of eleven children.[32]]

March 16
We received our report cards and I made As on every subject.

March 17 Saturday
Went to "High Point" this morning and got a blue georgette dress. Came back to Asheboro this afternoon and saw Edith Brower & Edith McDowell. [High Point is about twenty-five miles northwest of Seagrove in Guilford County. In 1930, High Point had a population of 36,745 people; Asheboro, 5,021.[33]]

March 18
Went to Sunday school this morning. I visited Vada this afternoon and we, with Lane, went to Star, Biscoe & Candor. [Star, Biscoe, and Candor are small towns south of Seagrove located in eastern Montgomery County.]

March 19
Mr. O'Quinn and Arthur Auman had a fight to-day in school. [Arthur Wilson Auman (1913–93), a son of Alpheus Auman, was Mary's first cousin; Arthur Claude Auman (1912–67), a son of John Auman, was Mary's second cousin. It is not clear today which Arthur engaged in the fight.]

March 20
Today we watched the boys practice playing ball.

March 21
Vada and I studied to-day for the final examinations on English, which we will have Friday.

March 22
I am spending the night with Vada. We had much fun trying on Thyra Wright's dresses and playing with pillows. [Thyra Wright, a teacher at Seagrove School, was a daughter of Frank M. Wright, the U.S. postmaster at Asheboro.[34]]

March 23
To-day Seagrove played her first base ball game of the season with Shiloh and was defeated by score of six to two. [The Shiloh School was located several miles northeast of Seagrove.]

March 24 Saturday
Raked the flower garden this morning.

March 25
Wade Harris, Leslie Auman, Howard, and myself played parlor croquet this afternoon. [Wade Harris, age about twelve, was the son of Arthur and Lula Harris. Arthur was the cashier at the Bank of Seagrove. Mary's father was the president of the bank. The Harris family lived across the street from the Auman residence.[35]]

Image 15: The old Seagrove Bank building (built about 1921)
houses a pottery today (2007).

March 26
Read "Pride and Prejudice" to-day. [A novel written by Jane Austen.]

March 27
Went to Star to-night and saw "Rosetime" a musical comedy. ~~Jerry Hunter~~ (Paul Scarborough) was the hero. [This is a reference to a student play at Star High School. It is unknown why Mary crossed out the name Jerry Hunter.]

March 28
Had a class meeting to-day and discussed our graduating exercise.

March 29
Mabel took the Mumps to-day.

March 30
Our graduation announcements came to-day.

March 31 Saturday
Daddy and I stayed up until twelve o'clock to-night listening to "an old time Barn Dance" over the radio. [*The Courier* reported in March that Mary's father, Frank Auman, "is building a large addition to his lumber plant here and also putting in a new dry kiln."[36]]

April 1928

April 1
Went with Grandpa, Grandma & Aunt Hattie to-day to Why Not. Martha Graves and I "got tickled" in church. [Hattie Dennis was Charlie Luck's oldest daughter.]

April 2
Went with Grandma down to John Yow's this afternoon. [Mary's "grandma" was Fannie Luck, Charlie Luck's second wife. His first wife, Mary Luck (née Allred, 1860–1912)—the mother of all of his children—died of cancer in 1912. The family buried Mary Allred Luck at the Hopewell Friends (Quaker) Church in southern Randolph County where Charlie joined her in 1932; they buried Fannie Luck at the Old Asheboro City Cemetery. John and Lillie Yow, ages about forty-three and thirty-six respectively, were farmers living in Richland Township near Seagrove.[37]]

Image 16: Mary E. Luck, Charlie Luck's first wife and the mother of Mattie Auman, Bertha Auman, Belle Cornelison, Mamie Hughes, Hattie Dennis, Ivey Luck, and Everett Luck.

April 3

Received invitation this afternoon to the Junior-Senior banquet to be given April 10. [This is a reference to the Seagrove High School Junior-Senior Banquet.]

April 4

Vada & I went with Fred Auman on the school bus this afternoon & Vada got her head bumped when we passed a ridge in the road. [At the time, North Carolina hired students to drive their school buses. Fred Auman (1907–89), age about twenty at this time, was Mary's second cousin. He was one of the eleven children of John and Della Auman, farmers, who lived about four miles west of Seagrove in Union Township.[38]]

Image 17: Fannie, Charlie Luck's second wife, about 1888.

April 5
To-day the teachers decided not to give their play, "Eyes of Love" to-morrow night on account of Mr. O'Quinn and Ben Auman. [Benjamin Franklin Auman (1899–1982) was a salesclerk at a hardware store in Biscoe (Montgomery County) in 1930. It is unclear today what happened between Mr. O'Quinn and Ben Auman, but since Ben was twenty-nine years old in 1928, it is unlikely that it had anything directly to do with matters at Seagrove School where O'Quinn was a teacher. O'Quinn lived in Star, a small town about five miles north of Biscoe.[39]]

April 6
To-day our society planned an Easter Program to give to-night.

April 7 Saturday
Howard & Mr. White went to Asheville & Gren. S.C. Raeford Williams gave the senior class a party to-night. From his house, we walked to "Mineral Spring." ["Gren." is probably an abbreviation for Greenville. See entry for January 10, 1928, for information on Raeford Williams.]

April 8
Attended Easter Services here to-day. This afternoon I hid eggs for Louise, Susan, Helen, Jean and Earnest King. [On the King family, see entry for February 25, 1928.]

April 9
Our Science Class went to "Black Ankle" to-day on a field trip. Saw gold mine & tar kiln. Took Doc Martin & Shuley's pictures. [Black Ankle is a rural community located about five miles southwest of Seagrove in Montgomery County. In the 1920s, it was a haven for bootleggers. In the nineteenth century, the area produced tar and turpentine. The Black Ankle Gold Mine had enjoyed a moderate success in previous decades. Dave Cornelison owned land adjacent to the Black Ankle Gold Mine. Around 1900, he sold it to the owners of the mine for a handsome profit. In the antebellum decades of the nineteenth century, the Piedmont area of central North Carolina produced gold in quantities great enough to induce the United States to establish a government mint at Charlotte.[40]]

April 10
Went to the Junior-Senior banquet here to-night. Mr. White took mumps this morning.

April 11
It rained all day and we got out of school at 1:00. Howard & Fred went to sleep in the schoolroom.

April 12
Lane, Vada & I went to Asheboro to get Miss O'Quinn a birthday present for Senior Class.

April 13
To-day the Senior class with Miss Thyra Wright went to the "Gap." Vada & I went with Fred on school bus and got my head bumped. [The "Gap" is a breach in the Uwharrie Mountains through which wagon traffic passed in the antebellum era on the trade route between Salem in Forsyth County to the west and Fayetteville in Cumberland County to the east. In the 1850s, a

company chartered by the state of North Carolina built a plank road along this route. The Gap is located about one mile south of Seagrove School.[41]]

April 14 Saturday
Read "Last of Mohicans" to-night. [*The Last of the Mohicans* is a novel written by James Fennimore Cooper.]

April 15
Stayed at home all day, as it rained and was very cold.

April 16
Vada & I went to the branch below the schoolhouse this afternoon. We gathered violets and new, tender, leaves.

April 17
Vada spent the night with me. I am sixteen today—found out that I was to have "The Last Will & Testament" in graduating exercise & Vada "Valediction."

April 18
Vada & I went with Fred [Auman] & Elijah [Lucas] on the school bus this afternoon. Mr. Covelough from Elon [College] came to see Howard & I. [G.D. Colclough was an assistant business manager at Elon College.[42]]

April 19
Went to a party tonight given for the S.H.S. Seniors by Mrs. Lonnie King. [Lonnie King was a cross-tie inspector for the railroad.[43]]

April 20
Voted on our class superlatives this morning. I was voted the most studious & most musical & the flirt.

April 21 Saturday
Went to High Point to-day. Martha Graves went with me & got her graduation dress & slippers.

April 22
Went to my grandfather's this afternoon to take Aunt Hattie. As the road was very muddy, the car slid in the side ditch. Mrs. Elsie King has new daughter Dorothy. [On the Elsie King family, see entry for February 25, 1928.]

April 23
Took final exam on History today.

Image 18: Class of 1928, the first class to graduate Seagrove High School. First row (*left to right*): Maple Lawrence, Alberta Auman, Alta Matthews, Vernitia Stutts, Martha Graves, Mary Auman, Vada Graves. Second row: Bill Matthews, Walter Macon, Lane Russell. Back row: Elijah Lucas, Fred Auman, Howard Auman, Harwood Graves.

April 24

Vada and I went to the stream below the schoolhouse this morning. The scenery is very beautiful. [The peaceful stream that the girls admired has a bloody history. Its source was nearby Gollihorn Springs, which local residents named after Alpheus Gollihorn, a member of a pro-Union gang of deserters and draft-dodgers who terrorized loyal Confederates during the Civil War in the Randolph-Moore-Montgomery County area. A company of Confederate soldiers staked and shot Gollihorn near the springs soon after his capture on March 22, 1865.[44]]

April 25

We scattered reeds on our floor this morning and the janitor wouldn't sweep it so we had to. [H. Duckery "Duck" Smith was the first janitor hired by Seagrove School. Smith was married to one of Mary's great aunts. See entry for January 14, 1928.]

Image 19: Howard Auman at Pilot Mountain, 1928.

April 26
Our science class walked to "Coles Pottery" this afternoon and Philmore
Graves brought us back. [The J.B. Cole Pottery, owned and operated by Jason
B. Cole, his son Waymon, and his daughter Nell, was located in the northwest
corner of Moore County about three miles south of Seagrove. In 1928, Nell
married Philmore "Phil" Graves. In the 1930s, the J.B. Cole Pottery became
commercially the most successful pottery in the area.[45]]

April 27
Sent my invitations off to-day.

April 28 Saturday
The Senior Class went to Pilot Mountain on picnic. After we had climbed mt.
& ate dinner we went to the Blue Ridge in Virginia [Pilot Mountain State Park
is located about twenty-two miles north of Winston-Salem, North Carolina.]

April 29
I spent to-day with Vada.

April 30
Received a present from Gola Lowdermilk, my fifth grade teacher.

May 1928

May 1
I spent to-night with Vada. We read magazines, played ball, and studied.

May 2
Received a present from Carl Peters of Appalachia, Virginia, this afternoon. [Carl, age about fifteen, was a son of William B. Peters, a physician in Appalachia, Virginia. His mother, Georgia, was a sister of the wife of A.C. Harris. On the Harris family, see entry for March 25, 1928.[46]]

May 3
Took final exams to-day on Literature and Manuel. Vada spent the night with me.

May 4
We had final exams to-day on Geometry and Geography. Learned that I had made As on all subjects.

Commencement

PROGRAM

Seagrove High School

Class Day Exercises
Wednesday Evening, May 9

Graduating Exercises
Thursday Morning, May 10

Commencement Program of the First Graduating
Class of Seagrove High School, 1928.
(front cover)

May 5 Saturday
Went to High Point to-day to get my graduating dress.

May 6
Commencement Sermon was preached to-day by Mr. Smith. I went with Martha G. to the Leach Reunion. Went with Ivey Boroughs to river.

May 7
Howard & I went to Asheboro after school and came back by grandpa's.

May 8
Practiced Class Day Exercise this morning. School closed at 1:00 to-day as it rained very hard. Howard ate my dinner.

May 9
To-night I graduated from High School. To-day was the last day of school. [According to *The Courier*, twelve of the fourteen graduates of Seagrove High School in 1928 went to college. Of those, four went to the University of North Carolina (Howard Auman, Fred Auman, Elijah Lucas, Harwood Graves) and five went to Elon College (Mary Auman, Alberta Auman, Martha Graves, Vada Graves, Maple Lawrence).[47]]

Wednesday Night, May 9

Senior Class Day Exercises

Play: "Under Sealed Orders" by—
Three Witches
Lillie Smith
Della Mae Graves
Mary Tucker

Five Seniors
Lans Russell
Elijah Lucas
Vernitia Stutts
William Matthews
Walter Macon

Salutatory .... Harwood Graves

Class History .... Maple Lawrence

Class Statistics .... Martha Graves

Class Poem .... Howard Auman

History of Seagrove .... Alberta Auman

Class Grumbler's Remarks .... Alta Mae Matthews

Giftorian's Address .... Fred Auman

Last Will and Testament .... Mary Auman

Valedictory .... Vada Graves

Class Song .... Senior Class

Graduating Exercises

Thursday, May 10, 10 O'Clock

Song .... High School

Invocation .... Rev. J. C. Cummings

When Roses Bloom Again .... Seniors

Address .... Dr. W. S. Alexander

Presentation of Diplomas and Certificates
.... Prof. T. Fletcher Bulla

Benediction .... Rev. J. C. Cummings

Image 21: Commencement Exercises, Seagrove High School, 1928.

May 10
Today is Commencement. This morning—we received diplomas. I also got a certificate for being neither tardy nor absent. Afternoon—contests night-play "The Path Across the Hill." [A 1923 play by Lillian Mortimer. A school official announced during commencement that state education officials had accredited Seagrove School.[48]]

May 11
Obeira Leach came to see me this afternoon and we went to the dam in our pasture. We wrote our names on rocks.

May 12 Saturday
Found L— [illegible letters] to-night.

May 13
Lane, Vada & I went to Greensboro to-day to look over N.C.C.W. Had much fun about going to Danville. Went to church to-night here. ["N.C.C.W." refers to the North Carolina College for Women—currently, the University of North Carolina at Greensboro. In 1930, Greensboro had a population of 53,569 people.[49]]

May 14
Vada came to see me this afternoon. I went back with her and she ~~took~~ drove the car to her grandfathers.

May 15
Heard this morning that Aunt Hattie was very sick. Went up there this afternoon. Went to Star to a play to-night. [Probably a play by students at Star High School.]

May 16
Received a mesh bag from Louise Crawford this morning.

May 17
Mamma went to Grandpa's to-day to stay with Aunt Hattie. Mable & I kept house.

May 18
Vada came to see me this afternoon and we ate cherries. Took Aunt Hattie to High Point Hospital.

May 19 Saturday
Went with Ivey to High Point. Ate supper in cafeteria. [Ivey Luck was Hattie's brother.]

May 20
Went to High Point to-day. Stayed with Luey Davis in clinic.

May 21
One year ago to-day Col. Lindbergh arrived at Paris.

May 22
Alberta, Mildred, Mabel & I went to Hemp to-day to commencement. The play was "Out of Court." Stayed all night at Mrs. Lowdermilks. [Alberta and Mildred Auman were sisters. For more information on their family, see entry for January 22, 1928.]

May 23
Gilmer Auman came to Hemp for us this morning. [Gilmer Auman (1908–72) was an older brother of Alberta and Mildred Auman.]

May 24
Wade Harris took measles to-day. Alberta came to see me to-day & we played rook. [Rook was a card game introduced by Parker Brothers in 1906. It usually required a specialized deck of cards.[50]]

May 25
Mabel & I went to Wade's this afternoon & we played rook.

May 26 Saturday
Went to graduating exercise to-night at Asheboro.

May 27
Went to Asheboro to-day to spend a few days with Edith McDowel. Attended commencement sermon to-night [at Asheboro High School].

May 28
Went up town this afternoon. Met Penn Wood Redding & Davis Cranford & went to ride with them. Attended commencement address to-night. [Penn Wood Redding (1910–65) graduated from Asheboro High School in May 1928. Among the "class superlatives," his classmates selected him the best-looking boy in his class as well as "most attractive," "most original," and "best sport." He was president of his senior class and all of his classes starting with third grade. In the fall, he began his first year at Duke University. Penn Wood Redding was a son of J. Oscar Redding (1871–1954), president of a chair factory in Asheboro in 1920 and president of the Asheboro School Board in 1928. Davis Cranford (born about 1911) was the son of Chisholm C. "C.C." Cranford, the mayor of Asheboro and the head of Cranford Industries—a

firm that owned and operated furniture factories, hosiery mills, and other enterprises in Asheboro.[51]]

Image 22: Fayetteville Street School, Asheboro, North Carolina, built in 1909, renovated and wings added in 1924 and 1928.

May 29

Went to show with Buster Grimes. Edith M. & I went up town this afternoon. Met Joe Parrish & Henry Redding. <u>Saw Penn Wood</u>. Spent to-night with Edith Brower. [Joe Parrish (born about 1908) was the son of Melvin Parrish, an insurance agent in Asheboro. Henry Redding (1911–93) was the son of Thomas Henry Redding (1869–1918), president of Asheboro Hosiery Mills in 1910. Henry graduated from Asheboro High School in May 1928. In the class superlatives, Henry's classmates designated him as the "biggest eater" and the "laziest boy." They acknowledged him as a talented baritone. In the fall, he enrolled at the University of North Carolina at Chapel Hill. Buster Grimes's family identity is uncertain; he may have been a son of the owners of Grimes's Jewelry Store located on Sunset Avenue in Asheboro.[52]]

May 30

Ed. & I went to show to-night. Carl Rush & Dick McDaniels took us home in their new Ford. Penn Wood followed us. ["Ed." is a reference to Edith Brower.]

May 31

Went to Mr. Grimes's to-night. Edith & I were mad because we couldn't go to the movies. Joe tried to kiss us & we got in the loft of house. [Perhaps "Joe" was Joe Parish. See May 29 entry above.]

Image 23: Located at Fayetteville Street and Sunset Avenue, the Capitol Theater
served Asheboro from the early 1920s to about 1950.

June 1928

June 1
Went up town [Asheboro] this ~~afte~~ morn. Told Lawrence Rhodes good-bye.
Came home this afternoon.

June 2 Saturday
Went down town [Seagrove] this afternoon. Oberia, Maple & I sat on Mr.
Leach's porch & played cars. [Perhaps Mary meant "cards." Also on this day,
Howard Auman, Fred Auman, Harwood Graves, and Elijah Lucas—all 1928
graduates of Seagrove High School—spent the day in Chapel Hill looking
over the campus. Their high school teacher, Charlie O'Quinn, a graduate of
the University of North Carolina, accompanied them.[53]]

June 3
Attended Sunday school this morning. Went to Asheboro this afternoon to
see Edith Brower. Saw Penn Wood Redding pass.

June 4
Went to café [in Seagrove] this afternoon and got sherbet in Dixie cups. Ate
first new peaches this year.

June 5
Buster Grimes and Elmer Calicutt stopped to see me this afternoon. [Elmer Callicutt took part in the commencement exercises at Asheboro High School in May 1928. He was a star member of the Asheboro High football team. Rather than giving him a high school diploma, the school granted him a certificate stating that he had completed fifteen credits at the school. He earned the superlatives "most bashful" and "the quietest." In the fall, Elmer enrolled at Greensboro Commercial College.[54]]

June 6
Went out to the old school house.

June 7
Frank Leach came to-night. [Frank Leach, age about eighteen, was a son of Eli and Melissa Leach who lived across the street from the Auman household. Eli Leach was a cross-tie inspector for the Norfolk Southern Railroad. Frank was a student at the state School for the Deaf and Dumb at Morganton, North Carolina. He usually spent summers and holidays at home in Seagrove with his parents.[55]]

June 8
Maple Lawrence, Susan King & myself walked down to our pasture & gathered daisies & honeysuckles.

June 9 Saturday
Seagrove played a ball game with High Point this afternoon & won. Went to fiddlers' convention to-night. [The public schools in Seagrove, Star, and High Falls have held Fiddlers' Conventions annually from the 1920s to the present. High Falls is a small cotton-mill village on the Deep River in north-central Moore County. Several years ago, the High Falls Fiddlers' Convention moved to North Moore High School, and the Star Fiddlers' Convention moved to East Montgomery High School. Seagrove School still holds its annual Fiddlers' Convention on campus.[56]]

June 10
Edith McDowel came to-day to spend the week with me. Attended memorial services here.

June 11
Edith, Mabel & I walked to Martha Graves's [house] this afternoon. Harwood took us to Clinton Auman's pond. [The Clinton Auman and Graves's residences were located about a mile southeast of Seagrove in the Why Not community. Martin Clinton Auman (1890–1978), farmer, was Mary's third cousin.]

June 12
Went to Grandpa's this evening with Ivey.

June 13
Miss Lena Russell, Vada & myself went to Elon College to-day to make preparations for entrance this fall.

June 14
Went to ride this afternoon. Visited Aunt Si– [name unclear], Alberta, & Vada. Went to Aunt Belle's to-night & watched Juniors initiate new members. Paul Lucas & Mamie Boone, just married, came – [illegible word].

June 15
Went to High Point to-day.

June 16 Saturday
Edith & I planned to go to Lucas's fishpond this afternoon but Harwood couldn't go. Taught daddy how to play Rook to-night. [The Lucas fishpond was located about four miles west of Seagrove on the Bethel Lucas farm, near present-day North Carolina Highway 134.]

June 17
Aunt Hattie came home from hospital. Went to Grandpa's to-day. Went to the river with Ivey, Wade [Harris] and Aunt Mamie's children. Edith [McDowell], Mabel & I were poisoned. Went to [rest of phrase unclear].

June 18
Ate first new apples to-day. Gathered "sweet peas" this morning & ate gooseberries.

June 19
Went to High Point to-day shopping. Went to Wade's to-night & played rook.

June 20
Read "The Hollywood Girl" to-day. Euclid Auman married Lyde Bingham this evening. [Euclid Auman (d. 1953), Mary's third cousin, was the son of Jefferson and Elizabeth Auman, farmers who lived in Why Not. A 1927 graduate of Elon College and president of his senior class, Euclid Auman was principal of Stuart High School in Dunn, North Carolina. His bride was a teacher at Denton High School (Davidson County). Euclid's brother Clyde Auman (1893–1977), pastor at a Methodist Protestant Church in Enfield, North Carolina, performed the marriage ceremony. Euclid and Clyde Auman

would be teachers at Seagrove High School in the 1929–30 school year. *The Hollywood Girl* is a novel by Beatrice Burton Morgan, first published in 1927.[57]]

June 21
Today is very hot. Wade came over here to-night. We heard the back door open & got scared.

June 22
Went down in our pasture this afternoon and drove the cows home.

June 23 Saturday
Rained this afternoon. Read "Smart Set." Went to Wade's to-night and we played "Drowsy Waters" on piano. [Mary may have been referring to *The Smart Set*, a literary magazine that circulated between 1900 and 1930.]

June 24
Went to Pinehurst & Lake View to-day. Went with Fred, Martha & Elijah to school house to-night to entertainment by orphanage children. [Lake View was a local center of entertainment situated in eastern Moore County, about two miles south of the town of Vass. Pinehurst, a resort community noted for its fine golf courses, is located about twenty-five miles southeast of Seagrove. The "orphanage children" were from the Methodist Protestant Church Orphanage in High Point, North Carolina.[58]]

June 25
Went with Mr. & Mrs. Harris & Wade to Bessie Maness's home this afternoon to take their washing. Picked first blackberries this morning. I took washing to Mrs. Brower.

June 26
Elsie Kings children came over here to-night, and we played on the lawn.

June 27
Got invitation from Elmer Calicutt to go to Fort Bragg Sunday. [Fort Bragg, a large U.S. Army base, is located about fifty miles southeast of Seagrove.]

June 28
Went to High Point to-day shopping. Milked one of our three cows to-night.

Image 24: Six children of Franklin Auman (*left to right*): Frank, Alpheus, Elijah, Jasper, Sarah Anne Fields, and Jason, about 1920.

June 29
Made my yellow organdie dress to-day. Wade left for [Boy Scout] camp this morning. Ivey left for Myrtle Beach. [Myrtle Beach is a popular coastal resort in South Carolina.]

June 30 Saturday
Martha Graves spent the afternoon with me. We went down town and saw Vada. She has just got back from Mt. Gilead. [Mt. Gilead is a small town located about thirty miles southwest of Seagrove in Montgomery County.]

July 1928

July 1
Went to Aunt Sarah's to-day at Pleasant Garden and to "Ritters Lake." Made ice cream. Mae Fields came home with us. Aunt Bertha is 38 to-day. [Sarah Anne Fields (1870–1948) was a daughter of Franklin Auman (1826–1911) and a half-sister of Mary's father Frank Auman. In 1891, prior to her marriage to Charles Wesley Fields, she had been a student at the Asheboro Academy. Mae Fields was Sarah's daughter. Pleasant Garden is a community located in southeastern Guilford County; Ritter's Lake was a nearby amusement park. "Aunt Bertha" is a reference to Bertha Auman, wife of Lebbeus Auman.]

Image 25: Sarah Anne Auman, student at Asheboro Academy, 1891.
About two years later, she married Charles Wesley Fields of
Pleasant Garden (Guilford County).

July 2

Vada, Martha, Elijah, Fred and myself went to High Point to-night to Broadhurst Theater to see the "Big Parade." Lights went out. [*The Big Parade* is a 1925 MGM World War I drama (silent) starring John Gilbert.[59]]

July 3

Buster Grimes, Iris Wilson, & Elmer Calicutt came to-night for me to go to show at Greensboro. Mae [Fields] went home [to Pleasant Garden]. [Iris Wilson, age about twenty, was the daughter of Asheboro resident Troy Wilson, locomotive engineer for the railroad. She was a 1928 graduate of Asheboro High School. A star basketball player at Asheboro High, she earned these superlatives for a girl student: "most athletic" and "most indifferent."[60]]

July 4

Elmer phoned this morning & wanted me to go to Lexington with him. Went to "Clear Water Lake" this afternoon on picnic, then to Jackson Springs & Ellerbe [Springs]. [Mary had numerous Auman relatives living in or near Jackson Springs (Moore County)—all descendants of Jason (1850–1923) and Sarah (née Burroughs, 1857–1913) Auman, Mary's uncle and aunt. In 1880, Jason and Sarah Auman lived on a small, impoverished farm located near his father's (Franklin Auman, 1826–1911) home in the Auman's

Crossroads community in southern Randolph County. By the 1890s, he had moved to a farm located south of Jackson Springs on land where three counties intersected: Moore, Montgomery, and Richmond. There he found employment in the turpentine distilling business. Over the decades, Jason owned general stores at Norman (Rockingham County), Craigownie (Moore County) and Jackson Springs. He maintained a winter residence in Star (Montgomery County) so his children could attend the public school there. (Jason had two brothers living in Star: Braxton and Rufus Auman.) His main residence was at Craigownie where he engaged in farming, turpentine distilling, and sawmilling; there he also owned and operated, in addition to his general merchandise store, a cooper shop and a blacksmith business. Jason died of stomach cancer at his residence in Norman. His children buried him and Sarah in Jackson Springs at the Presbyterian Church cemetery. Clear Water Lake was located in the Jackson Springs community. Jackson Springs and Ellerbe Springs (Richmond County) were health spas that were popular in the nineteenth century. Lexington, the seat of Davidson County, is located about twenty-five miles west of Asheboro.[61]]

July 5
Frank Leach, Wade, Mabel & myself play[ed] rook to-night.

July 6
Wade came back from Camp (Boy Scout) to-day.

July 7 Saturday
Hal Walker was killed this morning in car wreck. Was drunk. Mary Tyson married John Deaton to-day. [Hal Worth Walker rolled his car containing two passengers about three miles south of Seagrove. He suffered no serious injuries. However, the wreck precipitated an "old nervous condition," and while being rushed from his home to a hospital, he had a fatal heart attack. He was thirty-three years old. His wife, Harriette, was a daughter of U.S. Congressman William C. Hammer of Asheboro. They had two children. Walker, as a lieutenant in the North Carolina National Guard, served in the Punitive Expedition against Pancho Villa, 1916–17. During World War I, he served in France as an officer in the U.S. Army. In September 1918, he suffered serious wounds by gas and shrapnel. Perhaps the "old nervous condition" was a result of wartime injuries. Walker had a short but interesting life. While serving in the U.S. Navy, he and a group of sailors had an audience with Pope Pius X at the Vatican in early 1914; around 1926, he participated in a charity boxing match held in Asheville, North Carolina, where he went three rounds in the ring with Jack Dempsey.[62]]

July 8
Our meeting began here to-day. I went to see Vada & we went to ride with Lane and met some boys from Mt. Gilead who came to see Vada. [By "meeting," Mary is referring to a five-day revival sponsored by the Seagrove Christian Church.[63]]

Image 26: Seagrove Christian Church, organized and built in 1915. Belle and Dave Cornelison and Mrs. Frank Auman were charter members.

July 9
Attended Church to-night. Anna & Samie Stewart visited Mabel & myself to-day. Frank Leach is in hospital. Mamie L. visited me this morning. [Perhaps this is a reference to Mamie Luck, a daughter of Charlie Luck. Anna and Sammie Stuart were Mary's cousins from Jackson Springs, North Carolina, both descendants of Jason Auman.[64]]

July 10
Howard & Leslie A. left this morning for Langley [Field], Virginia Attended church this afternoon & night. Mr. Johnson (J. Fuller) came home with us. He is a very interesting man. Told me lots about Elon [College]. ["Leslie A." is a reference to Leslie Wade Auman. (See entry for January 11, 1928.) Rev. J. Fuller Johnson of Fuquay Springs (Wake County) was holding a "series of meetings" at the Seagrove Christian Church that lasted three days.[65]]

July 11
Mr. Johnson spent the day with us. Attended church. He prophesized that Vada & I would get married just after we finished college.

July 12
Mr. Johnson left to-night. Attended church to-day, after which Mr. Cummings (217), Johnson (160 1/2), Obeira (134), Mabel (160 1/2), & myself (111) went to the store & was weighed.

July 13
Meeting closed to-night. Vada spent the afternoon with me. Mr. Johnson went home to Fuquay Springs to-day.

July 14 Saturday
Howard & Leslie came back from Langley Field to-day

July 15
Wade & Mrs. Harris left for Appalachia, Virginia, this morn. Heard Mr. Leach sing tenor to-night. Went to grandpa's to-day. Rudolph & Annie Grace & Lucy Davis were there. Rained very hard—ate cake. Took Dorothy King and went to Johnny Lucas's new house & to see Mrs. Spencer. [Mary probably heard "Mr. Leach sing tenor" at the first meeting of the Richland Township Singing Convention held at the Why Not Methodist Church. Choirs attended the convention from nine churches in Richland Township. Attendees came from as far away as Concord and Greensboro. Mary would reference going to this convention again two weeks later on July 29.[66]]

July 16
Clell Cooper came this morning. Went with him to schoolhouse this afternoon. Misses Morgan & Wren visited me. Vada Graves is seventeen to-day. [Clel Cooper, age about eighteen in 1920, was a carpenter boarding at the Russell Williams home in Seagrove. This was probably the same person as John C. Cooper, farmer, age about twenty-eight, living in Seagrove in 1930. By then, he was married with two children.[67]]

July 17
Played rook with Mabel & Mr. Cooper this morning. Mabel won. Went to see Vada & Alta Duke this afternoon. [Alta Duke was a friend from Chapel Hill visiting Vada. Alta's father, Addison Duke, owned an auto-repair shop.[68]]

July 18
Ivey got his new Ford to-day at Charlo—. Went to Harriet's to-night. Played leading each other blindfolded with Paul & Milta Von Cannon & Harriet's children. [Perhaps "Charlo—" is an abbreviation of "Charlotte." On Harriet King and her family, see entry for February 25, 1928.]

July 19
Went to High Point this morning. Got a Djer Kiss, old silver compact.—
Went with Vernitis & Elflata Stutts to singing to-night. [Vernitis and Elflata
Stutts (ages about eighteen and twenty-six respectively) were daughters of
William Stutts, farmer.[69]]

July 20
Collected all my old high school papers & compositions this morning &
cleaned up my room. Played rook with Oberia this afternoon.

July 21 Saturday
Vada, Lane [Russell], Martha [Graves], Elijah [Lucas], Alta [Duke], Fred
[Auman], Harwood [Graves] & myself went to Lake View this afternoon.
Came back to show to-night at Biscoe. [On Lake View, see entry for June
24, 1928.]

July 22
Went to Jackson Sps. to-day. Came back by West End and visited my first
cousin, Claude Auman & his family. Drove Buick. [Claude Auman (1878–
1939), farmer, was a son of Jason Auman, a half-brother of Mary's father.
Claude, his wife, Lillie Catherine Graham (1882–1969), and their children
raised peaches, tobacco, cotton, and other crops on their farm. At the time of
her death, Lillie had collected and saved thousands of letters, business records,
photographs, and other items relating to the Auman, Graham, Currie, and
other families dating from the 1850s to the 1960s. These records now comprise
the bulk of the Auman Family Papers on deposit at the Southern Historical
Collection at the University of North Carolina at Chapel Hill. West End is
located about four miles east of Jackson Springs in Moore County.]

July 23
Made pongee dress to-day.

July 24
Daddy is forty-five to-day & Mamma is forty.

July 25
Was vaccinated to-day for small pox.

July 26
Vada came back from Chapel Hill to-day.

July 27
Made two-tone pink suiting dress to-day.

Image 27: Lillie and Claude Auman with their children (*left to right*) Thelma, Glenn, Treva, and Clyde, 1913, West End, North Carolina.

Image 28: Claude Auman house, West End, North Carolina, built in 1915

July 28 Saturday
Went to see Oberia L. this afternoon. We, i.e., Oberia, Cecil, Beuford, Thelma, Ruth, Rachel, Doris & Nancy Spence went to their swimming pond. [Cecil and Beuford, ages about nine and eleven, were brothers of Oberia Leach. See entry for January 28, 1928, on the Leach family.]

July 29
Promised to marry Rankin Richardson to-night. Ha! Lane, Vada & I went to an old house covered with vines toward New Hope. Went to Why Not to-day to Singing Convention. Vada & I had much fun with Theodore Hulon & Elmer Gillis. Went to children's exercise to-night at Union Church. [New Hope Township was located about eight miles northwest of Seagrove. Rankin Richardson, age about nineteen, was a son of Joseph and Emma Richardson, farmers.[70]]

July 30
Today is Ivey's birthday (thirty-one). Read "How to Study."

July 31
Went to Wade's to-night & played rook with Cecil & Beuford. Ate grapes in dark. Tom Wallace gave me stick of chewing gum. [Tom Wallace, age about twenty-three, was a son of Lula Wallace, farmer.[71]]

August 1928

August 1
Am sick to-day from small pox vaccination. Martha Graves came to see me & Edith McDowell gave party to-night. [Illegible word(s)] go.

August 2
Am still sick to-day & Louise brought Dorothy to see me. Oberia also came. [Dorothy was an infant daughter of Elsie and Harriett King, Mary's neighbors. On the King family, see entries for February 25 and April 22, 1928.]

August 3
Better to-day. Got up this afternoon. Called Vada.

August 4 Saturday
Went to New Zion to-day to rally with Vada. Theodore Hulm was there. Vada & I came back with Lane & Reece/R- ["Reece/R-" is a reference to Reece Richardson, age about nineteen, brother of Rankin Richardson. See entry for July 29 above.]

August 5
Uncle Lebbeus & Aunt Bertha came to Grandpa's to-night. Went with Ivey up there to see them. Evelyn has grown so much—Vada & I came to store to-day. Dr. Sumner told Vada to have her arm dressed. [Evelyn Auman (1925–76) was the daughter of Lebbeus and Bertha Auman. Dr. G.H. Sumner was the chief county health officer, whose duties included looking after the health of schoolchildren, jail inmates, and the elderly at the county rest home.[72]]

Image 29: Bertha and Lebbeus Auman in auto at Frank Auman's residence, Seagrove, North Carolina, about 1916.

August 6
Went to ride to-day with Daddy, Mama & Mabel to Steeds. Went to Mr. Leach's to-night. Mary Walker told me about Elon [College]. [Steeds is a community located about five miles south of Seagrove.]

August 7
Cleaned house to-day.

August 8
Mr. Ross Charles bought out Seagrove Café to-day. [In February 1928, Mr. and Mrs. Ross Charles moved from High Point to Seagrove to buy and operate the New Gap service station.[73]]

August 9
Aunt Bertha & Uncle Lebbeus came down here this afternoon.

Image 30: Lebbeus and Bertha Auman, probably newlyweds, about 1913.

August 10
Played with Thomas and Samuel in swings at Uncle David's barn. [Thomas (1921–45) and Samuel (1921–1970) were twin sons of Lebbeus and Bertha Auman.]

August 11 Saturday
Went to Wade's this afternoon and ate grapes.

August 12
Preaching here to-day. Boyd Stout, a former schoolmate stopped to see me this afternoon.

August 13
The Vitraphone first come into use to-day. It enables one to hear the real voice of players in movies.

August 14
[No entry.]

August 15
Aunt Bertha and family left here this morning for grandpa's [i.e., they went to Charlie Luck's house]. Aunt Mamie came this afternoon. [Mamie Hughes (née Luck) was a sister of Mary's mother.]

Image 31: Charlie Luck house in 2007 (built about 1900).

August 16
Made a pink checked dress to-day. Went to theater to-night at Asheboro & saw "St. Elmo." [A Fox silent film melodrama released in 1923 starring John Gilbert.[74]]

August 17
Listened to radio and read poetry to-night.

August 18 Saturday
Went with Ivey to school house this afternoon to see ball game. Aunt Mamie left to-night.

August 19
Went to Sunday school this morning. Visited Alberta Auman this afternoon. Saw her new clothes. Got sweet gum in their pasture.

August 20
Uncle Leb & Aunt Bertha came back here to-day [from Charlie Luck's house].

Image 32: Franklin Auman, (1826–1911) about 1885 (*sitting, left*), with sons (*left to right*) Phillip (1859-1885)), Braxton (1857–1908), and Jasper (1852–1933). Franklin was also the father of Jason (1850–1923), Parena (1855–1869), Leacy Berry (1863–1894), Elijah (1865–1927), Rufus (1867–1946), Sarah Fields (1870–1948), Thaddeus (1878–1941), Alpheus (1880–1959), Frank (1883–1941), and Lebbeus (1885–1949).

August 21
Earnest Patterson came to-day to spend the week with us. We all went to Coles Pottery shop this afternoon. Got vase & small basket for my room. [Earnest Patterson (1910–99) was a son of John and Dora (née Auman) Patterson of Jackson Springs, North Carolina. Dora, a daughter of Jason Auman (1850–1923), was Mary's first cousin. On Cole's Pottery, see entry for April 26, 1928.]

August 22
Went to Leslie Auman's to-day with Uncle David & Uncle Lebs folks. Heard Al Smith's acceptance speech over radio to-night. [Al Smith was the Democratic Party nominee for president of the United States in the 1928 election.]

August 23
Went to party at Edith ~~McDowel's~~ Brower's to-night. Went to Asheboro this afternoon to have my teeth filled.

August 24
[No entry.]

August 25 Saturday
Dressed this afternoon and went down town. Took Evelyn and Thomas & Samuel to scuppernong vines. [Dave Cornelison had a small scuppernong vineyard between his house and barn.]

August 26
Went to Association to-day at Sugg's Creek. Saw Mamie Parks [&] Connie Miller. Gail & Maude A. came home with us. Went to Grandpa's with uncle Leb. [The Primitive Baptist Church held an "Associational" meeting at the Suggs' Creek Church that lasted from Friday to Sunday. Observers believed it to be the largest meeting of the Association in its history—from two thousand to five thousand persons attended the three-day event, which featured all-day open-air services and camping. Twenty-three Primitive Baptist ministers were present. Suggs' Creek Primitive Baptist Church is located about five miles southwest of Seagrove in Montgomery County. Mary's paternal grandfather, Franklin Auman (1826–1911), had been a member of Suggs' Creek Church. Connie Miller (1897–1994) and Maude Auman (1894–1947) were daughters of Jason Auman (1850–1923) and Mary's first cousins. Gail (Gayle) was Connie's son, age about five. Connie was the wife of Paul M. Miller, conductor for the railroad. They lived in Norman (Richmond County). Maude Auman lived with the Millers.[75]]

August 27
Stayed at Grandpa's last night. Went to ford with Evelyn & Millry Vuncannon and boys this morning. Came home this afternoon. [Mary is referring to a ford in the Little River near the Charlie Luck home place.]

August 28
Uncle Leb & Aunt Bertha left [for Langley Field] this morning at 4:00. Took pictures this afternoon. Went to Asheboro & had teeth filled. Wardrobe trunk came today.

August 29
Washed & pressed my clothes to-day.

August 30
Connie, Maude & Gail left [for Jackson Springs] this morning.

August 31
Went to High Point shopping, to-day. Went to Aunt Belle's to-night. Misses Ruth Fonce, senior in Radcliffe University & Dorthy French of Chattanooga Junior University [incomplete sentence]. [On the evening of August 29,

Mary's neighbor, Mrs. A.C. Harris, entertained the "Golden Star" Sunday school class. Games and refreshments followed devotions. Those present were Maple Lawrence; Ruth, Amos and Elsie Farlow; Vada Graves; Lane Russell; Reece Richardson; George Harmon; and Alberta, Mabel, Mary, Howard, and Fred Auman. Special guests were Ruth Founce and Anis La Charity. They were summer workers for the Congregational Church from Boston, Massachusetts, conducting Daily Vacation Bible School at the Seagrove Christian Church. [76]

Chapter 3

Elon College Days—The First Year

In the fall of 1928, Mary and four of her Seagrove High School classmates started their freshman year at Elon College (today, Elon University); her brother Howard and three of his classmates enrolled at the University of North Carolina at Chapel Hill. Elon College was a coeducational four-year institution of higher learning located about four miles northwest of Burlington, North Carolina. The Christian Church founded Elon College in 1889. The Christian Church was a Protestant sect formed in the late eighteenth century by a group of dissenters in North Carolina and Virginia, led by Reverend James O'Kelley, who seceded from the Methodist Church. (Mary's family attended the Seagrove Christian Church.) All boarding Elon College students were required to attend Sunday school and church on campus weekly.[77]

Mary roomed with her Seagrove High School classmate Vada Graves in West Dormitory. Other Seagrove classmates attending Elon College as freshmen were Martha Graves, Maple Lawrence, and Alberta Auman. Lena Russell, who had been a teacher at Seagrove School in the spring of 1928, returned to Elon as a senior; she would graduate Elon College as a member of the class of 1929. Lane Russell, Lena's brother, was a close friend and Seagrove High School classmate of Howard and Mary Auman. Elizabeth Slack, a friend and a distant relative of Mary from Hemp (today known as Robbins—a small town located about ten miles south of Seagrove in Moore County), also began her college career at Elon in the fall of 1928.

Mary attended Elon College for two academic years, 1928–29 and 1929–30. Her diary gives a portrait of daily life on campus. She often mentions the classes she is taking and her professors. However, Mary's primary interest lay in her social life. She describes life in the dormitories and the high jinks residents played on each other such as "salting" beds and "stacking" rooms.[78] Occasionally, she goes hiking or on a picnic. She makes frequent trips "downtown"—that is, to the small business district adjacent to the campus—and to nearby Burlington for movies, bowling, socializing with fellow students, and shopping. Except for certain designated hours in the afternoon when students were free to go downtown, the dean of women had to approve these trips before they could be undertaken. Mary sometimes went downtown or to Burlington without permission from the dean.

Mary went home to Seagrove most weekends. She often rode home with her brother Howard, who picked her up in his Ford on his way home from Chapel Hill. Alternatively, she would ride a bus to Asheboro via Greensboro. Mary seemed discontented at Elon College. She often complained in her diary of homesickness. Near the end of her first academic year, Mary had a dispute with her roommate, Vada Graves, and they went their separate ways.

College authorities strictly regulated social life on campus, especially relations between the genders. For example, they forbade smoking, dancing, dating, card playing, and the use of alcoholic beverages. They did not allow males and females to walk or talk with each other while going between classes or, with a few exceptions, to other campus activities. They required males and females to use separate staircases in classroom buildings; males and females had to enter and exit the library at separate points. They segregated seating in the chapel by gender. They allowed female students to leave the campus only once per week (except to go home), and then only with the permission of their parents and the college authorities. They permitted males and females to talk to each other or otherwise socialize only when in the presence of a member of the faculty or an approved chaperone.[79]

The executive board of the Elon College Woman's Association for Student Government strictly disciplined female violators of these regulations. All boarding female students were members of the association. Six students and the president of the association composed the executive board—all elected by members of the association. The penalty for a first offense was usually a simple reprimand. The executive board placed serious and repeat offenders on probation or restricted them to campus. The college president and the dean of women handled egregious violations that resulted in expulsion. During her two years at Elon College, Mary records in her diary numerous infringements of these social rules by her and many of her classmates, who were brought before "the board" and either "campused" or "probated" for days and sometimes weeks at a time.[80]

September 1928

September 1 Saturday
Miss Fonce & Miss French came this morning. Rained all day. Went down town this afternoon and bought some things.

September 2
Rained all day. Ate dinner with Aunt Belle. Read Miss Fonce's game book.

September 3
My first day at college! Attended freshman reception here (at Elon) to-night. (Room no. 66 in West Dormitory.) Rained all night.

Image 33: West Dormitory, Elon College, 1929, where Mary Auman roomed.

September 4
Still raining. Attended programs and lectures this morning. Prof. Velie played pipe organ. Met several new students. Saw moving picture to-night. [C. James Velie taught piano, organ, and music theory.[81]]

September 5
Wrote some. Selected course[s] this morn. Had them approved and I registered this afternoon. Went to auditorium & heard freshman address by Prof. Harper. [W.A. Harper was president of Elon College.[82]]

September 6
Began class work to-day. Had English, Education, and French. Had social hour at Y.W.C.A. after dinner. Ate grapes. [Y.W.C.A. is the acronym for the Young Women's Christian Association.]

September 7
All freshman girls went to Mabel Barrett's room, from Porto Rico & Ruth Baitson [from] Los Angeles, Calif. Had classes in Biology, Bible, and French this morning. Got letter from Mabel. Initiated boys to-night. Expected girls to initiate us to-night. [Mary was probably referring to Ruth Elizabeth Bateson of San Fernando, California.[83]]

September 8 Saturday
Harvey White married to-day in S.C. Had classes this morning. After lunch dressed and went down town. Went to Annual Faculty Reception to-night. I led the freshman line, followed by Huntley. [Here, "down town" refers to the small business district adjacent to the campus. Harvey White continued in his role as principal and high-school teacher at Seagrove School for the 1928–29 school year.[84]]

September 9
Attended Sunday school and church this morning. Had date with H.W. Hartley this afternoon from Pittsburgh, Pen. Louise Huff (Catholic) from N.Y.C. came to-night. ["N.Y.C." stands for New York City. Mary is referring to Louise "Hough" here, not "Huff." See Louise Hough's note to Mary at end of diary under "Memoranda." She was a freshman from Highland Falls, New York.[85]]

September 10
Went to Y.W.C.A. building to-day and played piano & victrola. Sat on lawn and watched squirrels and ate candy. School started at Seagrove.

September 11
Got letter from Aunt Belle. Had date with "Bubbles" at social hour. He let me ring the dinner bell. Met a boy from Madrid, Spain, & some boys from Cuba.

September 12
Went to library to-night. Heard Cuban boys sing. Went to Drug Store this afternoon and got orange ice. Talked with Margret Curtiss from Key West, Florida this afternoon.

September 13
Had gym this afternoon. Went to library to-night. Had lots of fun with Hinton Rountree and "Levi" at the card catalogue. [John Hinton Rountree was a sophomore from Norfolk, Virginia.[86]]

September 14
Had first laboratory period this afternoon. Learned to use the microscope.

September 15 Saturday
Howard & Elijah Lucas came after Vada and I this morning in his new Ford. Stopped in Greensboro and bought a pleated skirt. Grandpa & Geo. Im— [illegible letters] were at home.

September 16
Went to Sunday school this morning. Came back to Elon this afternoon.

September 17
Alberta Covington and Elizabeth Slack are sick to-night. Vada & I washed hair. Had pep meeting after dinner. Howard left for U.N.C. to-day. [Elizabeth Slack, age seventeen, was the daughter of Nixon and Swannie Slack who lived at Hemp in Moore County. Nixon Slack was a deputy sheriff. Alberta Brewer Covington was a freshman from Evergreen, North Carolina.[87]]

Image 34: Elizabeth Slack, freshman at Elon College, 1929.

September 18
Rained hard all day. Read paper in library. Went to social in Y.M.C.A. to-night. ["Y.M.C.A." is acronym for the Young Men's Christian Association.]

September 19
Rained to-day. Went to music building to-night and joined the choral society. Mama sent me a dress.

September 20
Took gym this afternoon. Vada & I are so sore we can hardly walk. We had much fun to-night eating tomatoes, peanut butter & crackers.

September 21
Saw advertisement of the fair at Asheboro. Heard Dr. Summerbell lecture here this morning. Had laboratory this afternoon. Read Courier & Greensboro Daily N. [News] to-night in library. [*The Courier* was an Asheboro newspaper. Martin Summerbell was a lecturer in church history.[88]]

September 22 Saturday
Went to Burlington this afternoon shopping with Charlotte Roberts. Saw Ester Ralston to-night in "The Spotlight." [A romance released by Paramount in 1927. Margaret Charlotte Roberts was a senior from Windsor, North Carolina. In 1930, Burlington had a population of 9,737 people.[89]]

September 23
Grandma is 60 to-day. Went to Sunday School & Church this morning. Socialized this afternoon with a boy (Bob Rustin) from Del. and the night watchman, who I went to church with to-night. His "old lady" talked to-night in church & tickled us. ["Grandma" is Fannie Luck, and "Del." is a reference to the state of Delaware.]

September 24
Got letter from Mamma this morning. Daddy stopped [by] on the way from Hillsboro. Got a card from Howard. [Hillsboro, the seat of Orange County, is located about twenty-three miles east of Elon College.]

September 25
Had our pictures made this afternoon for the college annual. Margret Curtiss, from Key West, Florida, who is very sick, was carried away to-night in the ambulance. Louise H. & Eliz. S. stacked Alberta C's room. [Louise Hough and Elizabeth Slack.]

September 26
We are all depending on the fair so much, that we can hardly talk about anything else & went to Y.M.C.A. to-night & had much fun with a boy that has had his hair clipped. [Mary is referring to the annual Randolph County Fair underway this week in Asheboro from Tuesday through Saturday.]

September 27

Got a telegram this morning saying that Margret Curtiss is dead. All the girls went on picnic to Moon Elon this afternoon. Ate wieners, sandwiches & drank coffee. [Moonelon is a tract of wooded land with a lake about one mile west of the campus used by the college community for picnicking, camping, and as a convention center.]

September 28

Elon played football game with State to-day. Score 57–0. Heard it broadcasted after finishing laboratory. [North Carolina State College (today, North Carolina State University), one of the state's engineering and agriculture schools, is located in Raleigh.]

September 29 Saturday

Evelyn's birthday (3 yrs. old). Went home [i.e., to Seagrove] with Vada's father this morning & stayed at the fair at Asheboro till night. Went thru the "Funnibarn." [Hiram Graves of Seagrove was Vada's father. Evelyn was the daughter of Lebbeus and Bertha Auman. The Randolph County Fair featured an exhibit building, a midway, a display of new automobiles, exhibits by Asheboro merchants, a prize farm animal display, arts and crafts exhibits, several "free acts" providing music and other entertainment, and fireworks every night at eight. Fair officials selected two "outstanding farmers" to set up individual farm booths that "were objects of beauty as well as of education." One of the farmers was Mary's uncle, Alpheus Auman of Union Township. The other was T.S. Lawrence of Seagrove.[90]]

September 30

Read funny paper this morning. Went to Sunday school. Went to Harriet's and Mrs. Harris's. Daddy brought Howard & Elijah back to Chapel Hill & Vada & I to Elon. [Harriet King, Lula Harris, Elijah Lucas.]

October 1928

October 1

Moved to Geo. Calslough's table this morning. Had Biology test. Went to meeting of Choral society to-night with Ed McPherson & Del. [G.D. Colclough was an assistant business manager at Elon College. Edwin Albright McPherson was a junior from Burlington, North Carolina.[91]]

October 2
Sent pictures off to-day to have more made. Went to social to-night. Talked to Hartly and came home with Rustin.

October 3
Dr. Burris delivered speech to-night at Seagrove for Al Smith. [Democratic Party operative J.T. Burrus, a medical doctor from High Point, gave a speech at the auditorium at Seagrove School in which he "addressed the political questions of the day."[92]]

October 4
Daddy came by this afternoon and brought us lots of fruit and candy. Went to social hour to-night. Talked to Highsmith & Jones. [Wyatt R. Highsmith was a sophomore from Greenville, North Carolina.[93]]

October 5
After Lab. this afternoon, Vada and I changed the furniture in our room. Ivey came after us and we went by Grandpa's and ate supper & took Aunt Hattie home with us.

Image 35: Sergeant Lebbeus Auman residence, Langley Field, Virginia, about 1930.

October 6 Saturday
Momma and Daddy left this morning about 4:00 o'clock for Aunt Bertha's [at Langley Field, Virginia]. Uncle Leb is very sick with rheumatism. [Sergeant Lebbeus Auman, who had been ill for over a month, was a patient at the government hospital at Fortress Monroe, Virginia.[94]]

October 7
Saw play to-night at church with Andrew "Out of the Road." Bob Rustin, hero. Went to Flag Springs this morning. After dinner went to Seagrove with Morgan, Wren, and Mabel and Ivey. Ivey & Ruby brought us back to Elon. A cop told me not to stand on fender of car. [Flag Springs is a Methodist church located about five miles north of Seagrove. Ruby Owen (1907–2000), daughter of Rufus and Martha Owen of Moore County, was a sister of the nationally recognized master potter Ben Owen (1904–83). In 1930, she and Ivey Luck married (see entry for June 25, 1930).[95]]

October 8
Had Bible test this morning. Lena Russell was baptized at a lake near here this afternoon. Clyde & Mary & Aunt Belle came. [In February 1929, members of the Psipheclian Literary Society elected Lena Russell, a senior from Seagrove, president of their association.[96]]

Image 36: Lena Russell, senior at Elon College, 1929.

October 9
Heard Suzanne Keener, coloratura prima donna sing here to-night. [Suzanne Keener starred in the musical *Love at First Sight* released by Chesterfield Motion Picture Corporation in 1930.[97]]

October 10
Vada, Louise Huft, Alberta Coventing, Sally Elders, and myself went to Elizabeth Slack's and LaRue Brown's room to-night and talked and cut up. [It was Louise "Hough," not "Huft," and Alberta "Covington," not "Coventing." Sally Crystabelle Elder was a freshman from Burlington, North Carolina.⁹⁸]

October 11
Found rules for our initiation that the sophomores put under our door early this morning. Had lots of fun. Al Smith came thru here this afternoon going to Greensboro to the Fair. [New York Governor Al Smith and his wife, riding on a special twelve-car train, sped through North Carolina from the Virginian line to Raleigh, and from there to Durham, Greensboro, Salisbury, and Charlotte. He did not stop in Burlington, where a crowd of about twenty thousand well-wishers cheered him along. Smith did stop for thirty minutes in Greensboro, where he rode in a motorcade through the town. A crowd estimated to be between twenty-five and sixty thousand greeted him. Observers believed that about four hundred thousand North Carolinians turned out to see the Democratic nominee for president of the United States as he passed through the state that day.⁹⁹]

Image 37: Carlton Library, Elon College, 1928.

October 12
After Lab. this afternoon Vada & I studied our lessons for Monday and to-night we washed some things and wrote letters.

October 13 Saturday
Harwood Graves came after us this morning. After I got home, I fixed a box to take to the box party to-night. After box party, we heard Republican speech. [Harwood's sister Martha was a freshman at Elon College.]

October 14
Stayed at home all morning. Went to Sunday school this afternoon and came back to Elon with Gilmer Auman & Clifford Lanier. Found our room stacked. [Gilmer Auman (1908–1972), a son of Artemus Auman, was Mary's second cousin. Gilmer's sister, Alberta Auman, was a freshman at Elon College.]

Image 38: Alberta Auman, freshman
at Elon College, 1929.

October 15
Highsmith teased me about wearing my "Al Smith" badge at the table. Wrote a letter to Aunt Bertha to-night. [On Highsmith, see entry for October 4, 1928.]

Image 39: Kress store on South Elm Street looking north, Greensboro,
North Carolina, mid-1930s.

October 16
Had a "pep" meeting this morning in chapel. Went to Elizabeth and Laure's
room to-night and took exercise and cut-up & talked with a boy from fenore
to-night. [It is unclear what place Mary is referring to by the term "fenore."]

October 17
Got a box of candy and chewing gum from Daddy this morning.

October 18
Had a pep meeting in chapel this morning. Some faculty members spoke. Pap
Eure, Hinton Roundtree, and Palmer Barrett, cheer leaders. [T.D. Eure was
a junior from Gatesville, North Carolina. David Palmer Barrett was a junior
from Ponce, Puerto Rico.[100]]

October 19
Had a mass meeting to-night in Y.W.C.A. All the foot ball boys made talks.

October 20 Saturday
Went on a special train with student body to Greensboro Stadium this afternoon
to ballgame played between Elon & University of Richmond. Pap Eure was
cheerleader. Met Louie Zeigler on train. Paraded thru Main Street headed by
two policemen. [Richmond devastated Elon 34 to 0. Louie Zeigler was a son of
Burt M. Zeigler, a salesclerk in a dry goods store in Birmingham, Alabama.[101]]

October 21
Went to Sunday school and church this morning. Talked to Louie Zeigler (from Alabama) this afternoon. He got hurt in ball game. Miss O'Quinn came to-night. Heard Blue Ridge program to-night in Y.W.C.A.

October 22
Went to library to-night and read magazines. My large picture came to-day that I had made for Howard.

October 23
Had date with "Sugar" Merrit to-night at Y.W.C.A. Moyd Fite and Pete ~~Richardson~~ Williams were there. [Moyd Albridge Fite, sophomore, age about eighteen, was a daughter of Craig Fite, a grocery merchant in Charlotte, North Carolina.[102]]

October 24
Elizabeth [Slack] and LaRue [Brann] had a quarrel to-night because Vada, LaRue, and I threw water in their room and pulled their shade down.

October 25
Had mass meeting to-night. Had Education test this morning under Prof. Johnson. Weather is cool to-day. [O.W. Johnson was a professor of education.[103]]

October 26
Elon played ball game with Guilford today, & [I] had date with Zeigler at the bonfire to-night. Louise Hough told us about New York to [remaining word smudged out]. [Mary is referring to Guilford College, a Quaker institution located near Greensboro.]

October 27 Saturday
Had English test this morning under Miss Hattie Brown. Vada went home with her daddy. Louie (Zeigler) went to Chapel Hill today & came back to-night, and we went to the show. [Hattie E. Brown taught Latin and English.[104]]

October 28
Went to Sunday school and church this morning. Had date with Louie this afternoon. Howard, Fred, Elijah, and Harwood came from Chapel Hill this afternoon. Vada came back to-night. [College authorities allowed male visitors on campus on Sunday afternoons.[105]]

October 29
Charlotte Roberts, Lois McFarland, Nannie Stout & myself went to
Greensboro to Carolina Theater this afternoon to see Al Jolson in "The
Singing Fool." Ate supper at Lois McFarland's home. Hopped ride from
Gibsonville. [*The Singing Fool* is a musical-drama with Vitaphone sound
released by Warner Brothers Pictures in 1928. It grossed more money
than any other movie in the 1920s. *The Singing Fool* was the first movie
ever to run more than a week at a theater in Greensboro, where capacity
crowds broke attendance records at the Carolina Theater. Lois McFarland's
parents, Leighton "Lee" and Myrtle McFarland, lived at 1313 Summit
Avenue in Greensboro in 1928. Leighton McFarland was president of the
Prox Mercantile Company. Margaret Charlotte Roberts was a senior from
Windsor, Virginia. Nannie Kathleen Stout was a freshman from Sanford,
North Carolina.[106]]

Image 40: Carolina Theater, Greensboro, North Carolina, 1931.

October 30
Went with Louie to auditorium to-night to piano & voice recital by two
ladies entertaining the Music Lover's Club.

October 31
Went to Nannie Stout's and Lois McFarland's room to-night and made candy
and had a feed.

November 1928

November 1
Heard that Eva Sykes had a baby.

November 2
Had monthly tests this morning in Bible and Biology.

November 3 Saturday
Tonight, Moyd, Gene, Mary Rawles, and myself went to Coach Walker['s] home and had dates with Pete, Watson, Zack & Zeigler. Elon played game with H.P. [High Point College]. We slipped off while everyone was at the show. [Mary and the other girls broke the *Elon College Handbook* regulations against dating by "slipping off" with the boys to Coach Walker's house without permission from the dean of women to do so. Mary Rawles Jones

Image 41: *From left*, Mabel, Howard, and Mary Auman, about 1920.

was a sophomore from Holland, Virginia. Douglas C. Walker, hired in 1927, was Elon College's first professional coach.[107]]

November 4
Attended Sunday school this morning and made a short talk on "Habit." This afternoon Moyd Fite, "Gene" Grab & I were mad at Pete, Watson & Zeigler. Zeigler asked for a date to-night but Moyd wouldn't let me go. Talked to Moyd, Gene, Nannie [Stout] & Lois [McFarland] to-night. Vada went to church.

November 5
Felt badly all day. Zeigler wouldn't speak. Al Smith & Hoover made their last speeches over radio to-night.

November 6
Got a note in the library to-night from Zeigler. Herbert Hoover was elected president to-night. Al Smith was defeated.

November 7
Zeigler called me to-night, and we socialized on the walk a long time. He is leaving to-morrow for Miami.

November 8
The football team left this morning for Miami, Fla., where they will play the University. Couldn't go with Zeigler to the train on account of French class.

November 9
Had Lab. this afternoon, studied morning glory and Spirogyra. Received Bible test papers—made 80. Vada had her hair cut this afternoon.

November 10 Saturday
We all went home this morning. Martha [Graves] & I were afraid that Howard was not coming. Went to Negro Minstrel [Show] at [Seagrove] Schoolhouse to-night & program by Glee Club. The [Elon College] football team played Miami to-day and "WON" [!]

November 11
Howard, Mabel and I went to Grandpa's this morning and got walnuts & hickory nuts. They came back with us [to Seagrove]. We all came back with Lane [Russell to Elon College] this afternoon. Got card from Zeigler & letter from B—.

November 12

Mother Ring had a hedge set out around the dormitory to-day. Leaves on trees are nearly gone. [Mrs. Francis J. Ring was the superintendent of grounds at Elon College.[108]]

November 13

The football team got back at 1:55 this PM. Met Zeigler at the train. Had date with him to-night.

November 14

A man representing the "Theodore Presser Co." talked and sang for us in Chapel this morning. He sang "Sunshine & Rainbow Valley" & several more. The Clio & Phylogian Societies debated to-night. [The Theodore Presser Company is a publisher and distributor of music.]

November 15

Had date with Zeigler to-night. We socialized at the gate. K.H.G.B. Mr. Cannon, Coach Walker and the football boys told us about their trip in chapel. [C.M. Cannon was both the college registrar and the manager of athletics. It is unclear what Mary was referring to by the letters "K.H.G.B."[109]]

November 16

The football team left at 7:30 this morning for Emory Va. where they will play a game to-morrow. Went on a field trip in Biology this PM. Psykaleon & Psyphelian Societies debated to-night. Mrs. Walker said to-night that Dean Savage had found out that we went to her house & had dates. We are all scared. [Louise Savage, age about thirty-one, was dean of women and head librarian at Elon College. She had a Bachelor's degree from the University of Virginia and had been a librarian for six years at Fort Loundon Seminary before school authorities hired her at Elon College in 1925. Her employment at Elon ended in the summer of 1930. (For more on Savage, see entry for April 1, 1930.) Emory and Henry College is located at Emory, Virginia. Mary is referring here to the Psykaleon and Philologian Literary Societies.[110]]

November 17 Saturday

Had English class this Morn. Lonesome this afternoon as about everyone has gone off. Seagrove boys and girls played basketball with Franklinville and won both games. [Franklinville is a cotton-mill village on the Deep River about five miles northeast of Asheboro.]

November 18

Attended Sunday school and church this morning. Bernice Auman and the boys from Chapel Hill came this afternoon. The freshmen class gave program in C.E. Went with Zeigler. [Bernice Auman (1903–67) was the son of John Roe and Della Victoria Auman, farmers who lived in Union Township west of Seagrove; he was Mary's second cousin. On Bernice Auman's marriage to Swannie Reynolds in 1929, see entry for June 18, 1930.[111]]

November 19
Moyd [Fite], Lois [McFarland], Dolly, and Margerie are before the faculty for night riding. Daddy came this afternoon from Orange County and brought us fruit. [College authorities forbade male and female students to ride in automobiles together except on picnics and special occasions. Women students convicted of hitchhiking faced expulsion. It is noteworthy that in her entry for October 29, 1928, Mary wrote that she "hopped a ride from Gibsonville."[112]]

November 20
Went to social hour to-night. Talked to "Speck" Stevenson and "Knight" till Zeigler came. Lane sent Vada a mirror souvenir from Asheville. He is coming back [to Seagrove] to-morrow.

November 21
Prof. Powell talked to us this morning about choosing a good course. Read magazine in library to-night & attended choral rehearsal. [T.E. Powell taught biology and geology.[113]]

November 22
Went to social hour to-night [&] played domino[es] with Pitts Vicar. Heard that Mr. Farlow & Mrs. Harmon are married. [Dominoes is a game for two to four players utilizing rectangular blocks with dots on them that match the dots on dice. The game probably originated in China in the twelfth century A.D. By the eighteenth century, it had made its way to Western Europe.[114]]

November 23
"The Show Off," play by the expression department was given here to-night. [The Show Off is a 1924 play by George Edward Kelly (1887–1974).[115]]

November 24 Saturday
Vada & I went to Greensboro this afternoon and got red & blue dresses and shoes. Came back for show to-night. Ate candy.

November 25
Went to Sunday school & church this morning. Had date with Zeigler this afternoon. He told me about Birmingham, his hometown, and Florida. Vada is feeling spry to-night & she is cutting up.

Image 42: T.E. Powell, professor of biology and geology, Elon College, 1929.

November 26
[No entry.]

November 27
Didn't go to social hour.

November 28
Getting ready for Thanksgiving. Studied lessons and bathed to-night.

November 29
Social hour all day. Zeigler was with Anna Virginia Britt. Won ball game with Lenior-Rhyne this afternoon. Thanksgiving dinner to-night. Philologian entertainment to-night. [Lenior-Rhyne, a small private liberal-arts college associated with the Lutheran Church, is located in Hickory, North Carolina. Anna Virginia Britt was a freshman from Holland, Virginia.[116]]

November 30
Howard & Mabel came after me this morning. Stopped in Greensboro. Went down town [Seagrove] this afternoon with Oberia. Went to Aunt Belle's to-night. Studied Biology.

December 1928

December 1 Saturday
Rained all morning. Mabel made me a cake. Went to Aunt Belle's to-night & listened to radio.

Image 43: Belle and Dave Cornelison house, Seagrove, North Carolina, about 1920; Dave is sitting on porch at left.

December 2
Went to Sunday school this morning. Edith B. & McDowell came. Came back [to Elon College] with Gilmer, Reed & Fred. Alberta drove. [Edith Brower and Edith McDowell, Gilmer Auman, Reed Richardson, Fred Auman, and Alberta Auman.]

December 3
Had Biology test this morning. Made 90. Louie won't speak. Began eating at new table this morning (Miss Raine's). [Sue Raines taught "household arts."[117]]

December 4
Made up lab. that we missed Friday. Shot water on D. Knight with a medicine dropper. Had date with him to-night in Y.M.C.A. Played dominoes. Talked with Watson & Rountree on stairs. [Dennis Knight was a freshman from Stokesdale, North Carolina.[118]]

December 5
Made up English test this afternoon in Miss. Brown's office. Attended choral rehearsal to-night. Vada has just promised to set me up every day next week if I make the best grade on English & visa versa.

December 6
Went to social hour to-night. Talked to "Capo," a Cuban. [Michael Lexto Capo was a freshman from Matanzas, Cuba.[119]]

December 7
Attended choral rehearsal to-night.

December 8 Saturday
Dressed this afternoon & went down town. Played piano in café. Saw officers take a Negro to jail. Saw "Shepard of the Hills" to-night at show. [The small business district adjacent to the campus is the "down town" Mary is referring to here. *The Shepherd of the Hills* is a melodrama issued by First National Pictures in 1928 starring Alec Francis and Molly O'Day.[120]]

December 9
Attended Sunday school & church. Had date with Ziegler this afternoon. Went down town. The Choral society gave a program to-night. Ruby, Lillian & Lacy C. came.

Image 44: Sunset Avenue, Asheboro, NC, about 1932

December 10
Got a letter from Mamma saying that school had closed because of the flu at Seagrove.

December 11
Talked to Bob Rustin & Lacy to-night. [Thomas Robert Rustin was a senior from Dover, Delaware.[121]]

December 12
Had Biology Lab. test this afternoon. Louise Hough studied Eng. with us to-night. Roe Allen died to-day.

December 13
The Press Association of High Schools came to-day. T.S. Ferree was here. Talked with him to-night at social hour. All schools in state closed on account of flu.

December 14
Last day of school before Christmas. Exams begin to-morrow. Went to Burlington this afternoon & got x-mas presents & got dress. Talked about closing school to-night on account of flu.

December 15 Saturday
Had final exam on English this afternoon. Went to first basketball game here to-night in Boy's Gym. Elon beat Raleigh.

December 16
Rankin Richardson, George Harmon, & Fred Auman came this afternoon. Louise Hough spent the night with Vada & I. About one o'clock to-night we found that we would go home to-morrow. [George Harmon, age about twenty-four, was a son of David Harmon, a farmer living near Seagrove in 1910.[122]]

December 17
Had test on Education this morning. Made 85. Howard, Gilmer & Lane came after us. Didn't tell L. good-by. Mabel has flu. ["L" is probably a reference to Louie Ziegler.]

December 18
Cleaned up and decorated for Christmas this morning. Got card from Louie.

December 19
Went to church to-night with Fred & practiced for entertainment. ["Fred" is probably a reference to Fred Auman.]

December 20
Went to High Point this afternoon to do some shopping. Sent Louie a card. Rained all day.

December 21
Decorated the church this afternoon. Gave program there to-night. Carl Lemonds was drunk and tickled us so.

December 22 Saturday
Mabel and I made a "big" cake. Went down town [Seagrove] this afternoon. Frank Leach came home. [Frank came home from the school for the deaf and dumb in Morganton, North Carolina, to enjoy the holidays with his parents in Seagrove. See entry for June 7, 1928, for information on the Leach family.[123]]

December 23
Went to Grandpa's to-day for dinner. Came back with Uncle David and ate supper with them to-night. Heard Christmas program over radio. Heard "Babe" Ruth speak. Vernitia Stutts was married to-day to Walton Brown. [George Herman "Babe" Ruth earned sports immortality as a home-run hitter for the New York Yankees baseball team in the 1920s. Vernitia Stutts graduated Seagrove High School with Mary in 1928. (See Image 18.) Vernitia and Walton Brown settled on a farm a few miles east of Seagrove in Brower Township.[124]]

December 24
Aunt Belle & Mable dressed turkey. Oberia, Mabel & I had much fun playing with balloons. Frank Leach gave me his picture.

December 25
Fixed dinner for Grandpa's folks, Uncle David & Aunt Belle, Ivey, and Uncle Jasper. Went to Mr. & Miss O'Quinns party for our class tonight. [Jasper Auman (1852–1933) owned and operated a general merchandise store in Seagrove. In 1918, Jasper built his store adjacent to Frank Auman's store on Main Street.]

December 26
Daddy went hunting with his new dog Mutt to-day & got several birds. Listened to radio to-night. [Frank Auman and his son Howard were avid quail hunters.]

Image 45: Jasper Auman store in 2007 (built about 1918). Today, the store houses a pottery business. The owners relocated the store from its original location in downtown Seagrove to a site across from the Sun Trust Bank.

December 27
Got card from Rodriguez [in] Cuba to-day and from Louise [Hough in] New York. Read story "Eve Goes On" to-night. Went to see Alberta & Mildred and we made candy & went to ride on truck.

December 28
Mabel, Oberia & I made candy.

December 29 Saturday
Went to High Point to-day and got me a black coat with possum fur.

December 30
Went to church this morning, [and] then went home with Vada with Rankin & Reese. Vada, Lane, & I went to the new dam below Mt. Gilead this afternoon. [Rankin and Reese Richardson. In the late 1920s, the Carolina Power and Light Company built the Lake Tillery Dam across the Pee Dee

River about five miles west of Mt. Gilead, North Carolina (Montgomery County).]

December 31
Went to school here to-day. Oberia was very funny. Wrote notes. Went to Asheboro to banquet for Randolph [County] students in college & to the show (with Harwood [Graves])—Lon Chaney in "West of Zanzibar." [An MGM melodrama released in 1928 starring Lon Chaney and Lionel Barrymore. The Randolph County Association of College Students sponsored the banquet, which the association held at the Methodist Episcopal Church in Asheboro at eight in the evening on New Years Eve.[125]]

Image 46: Ivey Luck's house in Seagrove in 2007 (built in early 1930s).

January, 1929

January 1
Howard left to-day for school. Played ball with Elsie King's children. [See entry for February 25, 1928, for information on the King family.]

January 2
Ironed this morning & fixed my clothes. Radio is very good to-night.

January 3
Grandpa's folks came this morning to wash [clothes] in Mamma's electric machine. Went back to school to-day with Vada. Went to social hour to-night.

January 4
Began classes to-day.

January 5 Saturday
Rained all afternoon. Went to Y.W.C.A. & played piano. Talked to Ziegler in Alamance Hall. No show to-night. Mabel is 15.

January 6
Went to church to-night & when we got back we found our bed full of salt. Vada found it first.

January 7
Poured water into La Rue's & Elizabeth's bed. [Larue Brann was from Brown Summit (Guilford County, North Carolina) and Elizabeth Slack from Hemp (Moore County, North Carolina).[126]]

January 8
Went to Burlington this afternoon. Saw Colleen More in "Lilac Time." Talked to Capo and Axpe from Cuba & Robert. [*Lilac Time* is a World War I drama released by First National Pictures in 1928.[127]]

January 9
Pete Williams came back to-day. Had pneumonia. Got our reports—(Eng. 90—F.d. 80—Biology 85—Bible 85—French 95).

January 10
Had ball game with Erskine [College] to-night. Lost. (30–17) [Erskine, a four-year college associated with the Presbyterian Church, is located at Due West, South Carolina.]

January 11
Dreaded Lab. this afternoon. Studied Hydra!

January 12 Saturday
Went to ball game here to-night with Guilford [College]. G. won. Score 28–25 Came back with a boy that sat beside me. Sororities sent out bids last night.

January 13
Attended Sunday school and church this morning. Wrote Mamma a letter after dinner. Went to church to-night. I had date with Lineberger.

Image 47: Sergeant Lebbeus Auman and his twin sons Samuel and Thomas
at Langley Field, Virginia, about 1922.

January 14
Had ball game to-night with Lenoir-Rhyne. Elon won 28–25. Went with
Andrews. Sat behind Z. Howard is 18 to-day. ["Z" is probably a reference to
Louie Ziegler. Twiman Glenn Andrews, a senior from Siler City, North Carolina,
was the only male in the 1929 annual with the last name of Andrews.[128]]

January 15
Faculty left this afternoon to go to grand opera in Greensboro. Went to ball game
between Sophs. & Fresh. Had social hour & I played checkers & domino[es] &
came back with Roberts (Georgia). [The San Carlos Opera Company presented
nine complete operas at the North Carolina College for Women's auditorium
in Greensboro this week. On this day, the matinee performance was *Tales of
Hoffman* by Offenbach and the evening show featured *La Tosca* by Puccini. The
operas were a grand social event for Greensboro.[129]]

January 16
Went to ball game to-night between classes. La Rue had money stolen.

January 17
Tony Sarz's marionettes were here this afternoon & to-night. Sat with Roberts & Jack Chandler. They are going to let their mustache grow & the one that grows the longer in 2 wks. gets me for their girl.

January 18
"Greater Elon Day" (Holiday) Socialized all afternoon with Davis Knight. Went to ball game. Dercis chased me & we played checkers & dominoes. Louie slept. Phykaleon Literary S. [Society] gave program to-night & we had big dinner.

January 19 Saturday
Went with Miss Chandler down town to drug store. Took pictures with "Speck" Stevenson. Operetta "Cinderella" at Seagrove to-night. Went to show to-night— "Little Shepherd of Kingdom Come." [A First National Pictures romance (silent) issued in 1928 starring Richard Barthelmess and Molly O'Day. The 1930 census listed Gertrude Chandler, age forty-six, as a housekeeper at Elon College.[130]]

January 20
Dr. Howsare preached this morning. Howard, Elijah & two boys came from the University. Scott & John Crael. Talked to Crael. Like him very much. Bood B—& Lane came. [Dr. Howsare was secretary of evangelism and life work for the Christian Church.[131]]

January 21
Cut Gym this afternoon & studied. Went to ball game to-night between Fred. & Burlington High School. Went down town after game with "Slack" & met Louie. Socialized at the gate. [These are probably references to Elizabeth Slack and Louis Ziegler. "Fred." likely refers to a high-school ball team.]

January 22
Made up lab. that we missed Fri. Studied earthworms. Had date with "Speck" Stevenson to-night. L. came in and went with Elizabeth. ["L." is probably a reference to Louis Zeigler.]

January 23
Looked up Education references this afternoon. Went down town to-night & Miss Savage left church & went down town & caught a crowd socializing. [This is a reference to Louise Savage, dean of women and head librarian (see entry for November 16, 1928). During posted afternoon hours, college regulations permitted female students to shop in the Elon College business district without a chaperone. However, while shopping, females could not fraternize with males.[132]]

Image 48: Louise Savage, dean of women and head librarian,
Elon College, 1929.

January 24
Studied biology to-night with E. Yates, Lillian Underwood & Christine
Wicker. Vada went to church. [Evelyn Yates was a freshman from Suffolk,
Virginia; Mary Lillian Underwood was a junior from Youngsville, North
Carolina; Christine Wicker was a junior from Sanford, North Carolina.[133]]

January 25
Had education test this morning, also biology test; Lab. this afternoon. Dr.
Hausare had illustrative sermon to-night with moving pictures in chapel
room.

January 26 Saturday
Had Eng. test this morning under Miss Brown. —Howard & John came from U.N.C. "Evangeline" was supposed to be given to-night but the film didn't come. [Howard Auman and, probably, John Crael. *Evangeline* (silent) is a historical drama issued by United Artists in 1929 starring Dolores Del Rio and Roland Drew.[134]]

January 27
Dr. Howsare spoke for us in Sunday school. Several joined the church here. Louie had date with D.W. Rained all afternoon.

January 28
Read Sunday's papers after lunch. Read "True Story." Cut chapel & ate breakfast. Roland Smith & Belle Wicker are mad. ["at each other" or, perhaps, "at me."] [Roland Smith was a sophomore from Fairfield, Alabama; Willie Belle Wicker was a junior from Sanford, North Carolina.[135]]

January 29
Sally Elder came this morning to study English. Voted on whether or not to keep Phisicli or not. Now (6:31) I am alone in my room. Vada is at social hour. [*Phi Psi Cli* is the name of the Elon College yearbook.]

January 30
Louie has the "Flu." Initiating B.O.B.'s to-night. Wrote Mamma a card. [B.O.B. stands for Beta Omicron Beta, a sorority on campus.]

January 31
Didn't go to social hour. Dread to-morrow.

February 1929

February 1
Studied the crayfish in lab this afternoon. Went home [i.e., to Seagrove] with Elizabeth Slack's daddy. Got there at 6:30 & ate supper.

February 2 Saturday
Mabel & I made cakes this morning. Went to Louise King's birthday party. Went down town this afternoon. Talked to Jim Comer & Joseph. [Louise King, age eleven, was the daughter of Elsie and Harriet King. (See entry for February 25, 1928.) On Jim and Joseph Comer, see entry for February 23, 1928.]

February 3
Went to Sunday school. Came home with Aunt B [Belle]. Went with Uncle David to store & got things to eat. Daddy & Mabel brought us back [to Elon]. V & I rode in rumble seat. Gee! but the wind blew.

February 4
Ate at Mrs. Johnson's table. Mildred Johnson is sick. Vada & I decorated the walls of our room with pretty pictures. [Mrs. C.C. Johnson worked in Carlton Library.[136]]

February 5
Snow on the ground this morn. Everybody snowballed. Took pictures. Made snow cream. Had no classes on account of Mr. Aubern's death. [There is no one in the 1929 yearbook by the last name of Aubern.]

February 6
Rained to-day and melted the snow. Marjory More left school. Elizabeth and LaRue moved into Moyd & Jean's room. Danced to-night. [Presumably Mary did her dancing clandestinely, since the student conduct rules in the *Elon College Handbook* forbade dancing on campus. References are to Elizabeth Slack, Larue Brann, and Moyd Fite. Majorie Moore was a sophomore from Dover, Delaware.[137]]

February 7
Got a letter from John Crael. Went to ball game to-night with Durham Y. [i.e., the Durham Y.M.C.A. team]. Elon won. Cut ban—

February 8
Studied Honeybee in Lab. to-day. Went to the Hall to-night—smoked. Stayed with B.O.B.'s to-night a while. [College authorities forbade smoking anytime on the first floor of the Christian Education Building (the social center for student life on campus) and on campus "in the daytime." Presumably, a student could smoke at night anywhere on campus except in the Christian Education Building. In light of the severe restrictions against every other vice, it seems unlikely that the authorities would permit smoking anywhere on campus at night. Nevertheless, the *Elon College Handbook* is not precise about the matter, so Mary may not have been breaking rules on smoking at night here.[138]]

February 9 Saturday
Washed my hair. OTK banquet—ball game with Catawba. 30–24—came back with Delock. [The Iota Tau Kappa fraternity held its "Radio Banquet" at 5:00 PM in the Y.M.C.A. Banquet Hall. It featured a five-course dinner

and radio music furnished by WPTF in Raleigh. Dace W. Jones was the Toastmaster. Catawba College, located in Salisbury, North Carolina, is associated with the United Church of Christ.[139]]

February 10
Skipped church this morning. Wrote to John Crael. Charlie O'Quinn, Lena & Martha went to Guilford. New girl from Sanford came. [Mary is probably referring here to Lena Russell and Martha Graves, students at Elon College from Seagrove. Charlie O'Quinn taught at Seagrove School. (On O'Quinn, see diary entry for January 2, 1928.) "Guilford" is probably a reference to Guilford College.]

February 11
Talked with "Lib" Davis & like her fine. Went to Burlington & saw Charles Rogers & Nancy Carroll in "Abie's Irish Rose." [A drama released by Paramount Famous Lasky Corporation in 1929.[140]]

February 12
Had date with "Lefty" Briggs to-night. He is a good basketball player but best in baseball. He has signed a contract to play with Detroit this summer. [Charles Vernon "Lefty" Briggs Jr. (1905–90) was a son of Charles V. and Renie E. Briggs, farmers in Gilmer Township, Guilford County, North Carolina. He attended Elon College from 1927–30 and was captain of the basketball team in 1928 and captain of the baseball team in 1929. In the last baseball season, he pitched eight winning games.[141]]

February 13
Got a Valentine from Howard & John. Vada & I made soup to-night. [Howard Auman, probably John Crael.]

February 14
Got a Valentine from Rankin Richardson & a letter from Mamma. [On Rankin Richardson, see entry for July 29, 1928.]

February 15
Studied tobacco worm in Lab. & had much fun in determining which end head was on. Studied clam also. Went to Valentine party here to-night with Bob McCloud from Fla. [Robert McLeod was a freshman from Barton, Florida.[142]]

February 16 Saturday
Rained all day. Went down town with Lib Davis & got $20 bill cashed. Payed Eiford for Phisicli & talked to him. Saw "The Ancient Mariner" to-night

with radio music. [*Phi Psi Cli* is the name of the Elon College yearbook. *The Ancient Mariner* is a 1925 silent film fantasy released by Fox Film Corporation starring Clara Bow and Earle Williams.[143]]

February 17
Had date with "Bob McLeod" this afternoon. Ivey, Rubie & Mabel came.

February 18
Vada [Graves] & Elizabeth [Slack] went to Burlington this afternoon without permission & were reported. Campused two weeks. Joined Psykaleon Literary [Society] to-night.

February 19
Went to Burlington this afternoon & saw Clara Bow in "Wings." Louie called me to-night & we walked around. He warned me not to be with "Lib" D. [Louie Zeigler and Lib Davis. *Wings* is a World War I aviation epic drama released by Paramount Famous Lasky Corporation in 1927 starring Clara Bow and Charles Rogers.[144]]

February 20
Mabel Barrett left last night for New York & is leaving there Thur. for Porto Rico, her home. Ground is white with sleet to-night. [Mabel Barrett was a freshman from Ponce, Puerto Rico.[145]]

February 21
Big sleet on ground. Got pictures that I had enlarged and a little tin pin picture. Moon looked so pretty on snow to-night.

February 22
Socialized & skated all morning. Had lots of fun ~~skating~~ snowballing tonight & this afternoon. Big dinner to-night & Clio Literary Society Program.

February 23 Saturday
B.O.B. banquet to-night. Dollie Williams took Louie. Saw "Black Butterflies" to-night. [A drama released by Quality Distributing Corporation in 1928 starring Jobyna Ralston and Mae Busch.[146]]

February 24
Went to Sunday school. Skipped church. Read, this afternoon. Vada went to church to-night. I wrote Mamma to-night & (C.O.L.). [The identity of "C.O.L." is unknown.]

February 25
Attended society to-night. Cut gym this afternoon & studied Biology.

February 26
Made up Lab. this afternoon. Studied frog. Played last basketball game to-night with H.P. College. H.P. won. Rained hard. Zeigler with Lois. [Mary is probably referring to Lois McFarland. H.P. stands for High Point]

February 27
Studied to-night for test to-morrow. Rained all night.

February 28
Had English test this morning. Read T.S. this afternoon. Lucile G. & I planned to go to Danville Sat. [Danville, Virginia, an important center of the tobacco industry, is located about thirty-five miles north of Elon College.]

March 1929

March 1
Had lab. Packed my clothes. Called Daddy & got permission to go to Danville.

March 2 Saturday
Lucile & I left this morning on train. Booster & Ralph met us at station. Met Leroy & Mr. & Mrs. Link. Went to show to-night & riding. Played rook. [This is probably Leroy Link, age seventeen, son of J.T. Link, civil engineer, who lived in Danville, Virginia.[147]]

March 3
Slept late. Doris & Nell came to see us. George called over phone. Went to ride with Leroy & Hobert Gilbert. Went to Reidsville. Rode lots in Forest Hills. [Could it be George Ward of Asheboro who called? Reidsville, North Carolina, is a small town noted for its tobacco manufacturing. It is located about twenty miles southwest of Danville, Virginia.]

March 4
Rained all day. We went up town [Danville] this morning shopping. Booster & I had lots of fun riding the elevator & trying on hats. We went to Dan (continued) River High School & got Hobert & went to show. He ate supper with us & we went to see "Skinny" & then to ride. They made up excuses to get out of school. We rode till late & took Hobert home. (President Hoover inaugerated to-day.) [*Skinny* is probably a reference to a Krazy Kat cartoon released in 1927 by Robert Winkler Productions and written by George Herriman.[148]]

March 5
Got ready to leave this morning. Leroy took us to station. Almost missed train. Waited long time in Greensboro. So sorry to leave there.

March 6
So blue to-day. Lucille & I would like to be in Danville. Rained lots.

March 7
Bob McLeod called for me to go to social hour with him. Vada went with Elwood Smith. Wind blowed so hard. [Elwood McCarley Smith was a senior from Brown Summit (Guilford County), North Carolina.[149]]

March 8
Got letter from Hobert this morning. Had lab this afternoon. Got ready to go home & wrote Hobert to-night.

March 9 Saturday
Went home to-day. Went down town. Fred [Auman], Lane [Russell], Vada & I rode to Asheboro to-night. Vada & Lane broke up.

March 10
Went to Sunday school this afternoon. Went to Aunt Belle's this morning. Came back to school.

March 11
Beautiful day. Wore new dress. "Lib" Davis probated rest of year for socializing with Royal Watson. Memorized classification in Biology. [Ural Warren Watson, a freshman from Sullivan, Indiana, was the only male with the last name of Watson in the 1929 yearbook.[150]]

March 12
Pleasant day. Larue [Brann], Vada & I walked to-night. Mamma ordered me an orchid dress.

March 13
Wrote personal essay in Eng. on "Early Rising." Miss Brown read it in class & I made 95%. Went to library to-night.

March 14
Got letter from Momma. Expected one from Hobert. Boys are practicing baseball & spring football.

March 15
Had Lab. this afternoon. Ate at Miss Ben's table. [Mary Ann Benn taught voice.[151]]

Image 49: Belle Cornelison, about 1930.

March 16 Saturday
Played piano in chapel this afternoon with Ruth Gregory. Saw funny show here to-night (air picture). Went with M. Johnson to Y.W. after banquet to-night. Came back with Riggins & we stole hyacinths. ["Y.W." is probably a reference to the Young Women's Christian Association. Margaret Sue Johnson was a senior from Elon College, North Carolina.[152]]

March 17
Had date with Riggins this afternoon. Went to church to-night. Had open forum & discussed "red book." ["Red Book" is the nickname for the *Elon College Handbook* issued each year as a guide to the rules and regulations students must live by on and off campus.[153]]

March 18
Went to Burlington this afternoon & got an orchid dress. Went with Edith Lockey & Gladys Spoon. [Edith Margaret Lockey was a senior from Newport, North Carolina; Glayds Irene Spoon was a senior from Elon College, North Carolina.[154]]

March 19
Hiked to Burlington this afternoon (4 miles) with E. Yates, C. Roberts & M. Coghill. Got blond slippers. Went to library to-night. Riggins walked back with me. [Evelyn Yates was a freshman from Suffolk, Virginia; Mabel Hunter Coghill was a freshman from Henderson, North Carolina.[155]]

Image 50: Downtown Burlington, North Carolina, early 1930s.

March 20
Got letter from Hobert this morning saying they were coming Sunday. Wrote Hobert & Momma. Went to library to-night & read magazines.

March 21
Beautiful day. Grass is getting green & golden bells & hyacinths are pretty on campus. Walked this afternoon. Dean Savage & crowd of us girls talked during social hour on steps.

March 22
Had lab. this afternoon. Trees are budding. Listened to beautiful music that boys played on French Harps to-night.

March 23 Saturday
Slack & I went down town & to Y.W. and played "Clayton's Grand March."
Show to-night "Romance of the Rogue." Came back with Rodrigues and
socialized at the gate. [*Romance of a Rogue* is a silent film released in 1928 by
Quality Distributing Corporation starring H.B. Warner and Anita Stewart.
A.A. Rodriquez was a sophomore from Havana, Cuba.[156]]

March 24
Cut church this morning (awful hot). Hobert, Leroy & Marshall came from
Danville this afternoon. Walked with Jack Chandler this evening after dinner
& went to church.

Image 51: Howard and Mary Auman, about 1926.

March 25
Beautiful day. Walked down town. Had social hour before dinner. Went to passion service with Leroy & came back with Andy. Sat on steps.

March 26
Had date with Jack C. Socialized on campus. Went to passion service. Trees and shrubbery are getting so beautiful.

March 27
Got letter from Hobert & pictures. Went to passion service to-night with Dofflemire & walked back with Fred Smith. [K.B. Dofflemyer was a sophomore from Ellston, Virginia; Fred A. Smith was a freshman from Hillsboro, North Carolina.[157]]

March 28
Had Eng. test this morning. Vada's grandfather died yesterday & her daddy came after her this afternoon. Lucille G. & I took pictures.

March 29
Howard came by for me at 12:30. Took Grace Wright & Howard Crotts to Asheboro. Colored Easter eggs. Saw good show at Asheboro to-night— "The Flying Fleet." [*The Flying Fleet*, released in 1929 by MGM, is a silent film about naval aviators in training starring Ramon Novarro and Ralph Graves. Grace Wright, age about eighteen, was a daughter of the postmaster in Asheboro and a sister of Thyra Wright, a teacher at Seagrove School. See entry for March 22, 1928, for information on the Wright family. Howard Crotts, age about nineteen, was the son of Ocia Crotts. The Crotts family operated a dry-goods store in Asheboro. The census listed Howard as a "sign painter."[158]]

March 30 Saturday
Mabel & I made cakes & helped Mamma cook. Went down town. Clifford Lanier came to see Howard.

March 31
Gave Mrs. Leach a surprise birthday dinner. Fred, Elijah, Martha, Alberta, Gertrude & I went to "Pinehurst." Went to Mrs. Harris' & made ice cream. Frank Leach came. Vada & Lane went up in an airplane.

April 1929

April 1
Went with Mabel to [Seagrove] school this morn. Ivey brought us back [to Elon College]. Elon played High Point [College] in Greensboro Stadium & won. Had Easter dinner & Psyphelion entertained to-night & date with Roberts. [Mary is probably referring here to the Psykaleon Literary Society.]

April 2
Didn't have English. Made up Lab. Changed to Dean Savage's table this morning. Read new magazines in library to-night. V. & I had lots of fun bathing in the dark.

Image 52: Mary Auman, about 1929.

April 3
Didn't have Bio. & Bible. Went to library & read magazines to-night. Daddy has built him[self] a new office. [By this time, Frank Auman's Seagrove Lumber Company, which he had purchased from Arthur Ross in 1926, was becoming a highly successful business enterprise.[159]]

April 4
Expression Dept. gave play here to-night: "Adam & Eve." Lilacs in bloom. Got a memory book with the Elon seal on it.

April 5
Today is so beautiful. Typical summer day. Played tennis. Walked down town after dinner to-night & Dan Long told me something. Forensic contest here to-night. [See entry for April 11, 1929, for information on Dan Long Newman.]

April 6 Saturday
Went to Burlington this afternoon & got a new hat (orchid) & pair of hose. Saw "Uncle Tom's Cabin" here to-night. Tulips are so pretty. [*Uncle Tom's Cabin,* a silent film released in 1928 by Universal Pictures, is a melodrama starring James Lowe and Virginia Grey.[160]]

April 7
Cut church this morning. Talked to Dennis Knight this afternoon. I'm going to hear Catherine Wade-Smith, famous violinist to-morrow night. [Catherine Wade-Smith won a Naumburg Violinist Award in 1925.[161]]

April 8
Got an invitation to a dance at State College from Howard Crotts. Got a [high school] graduation announcement from Paul Burroughs at Star. [On Howard Crotts, see entry for March 29, 1929.]

April 9
Had ball game with Wake Forest this afternoon & won (8–6). Went with Cagle & had a big time. Hiked in gym & got dogwoods & honeysuckles for our room. [In 1929, Wake Forest College was located in Wake County north of Raleigh. Mary is probably referring here to Lewis Cagle, a distant relative from Ether, North Carolina, a village located about five miles south of Seagrove. Lewis was a freshman at Elon College.[162]]

April 10

Got a card from Howard to-night wanting me to send him a picture for Alfreds Nazarene (Philipine). [Meaning & spelling unclear.] Got a box of lilacs from Mamma.

April 11

Made up an excuse to go to see John Lowry at the bank. Had a date with "Andy" to-night & went to debates (Elon & Lenoir-Rhyne). Talked to Dan Long & George Kelly to-night on doorsteps. [The following addendum to the April 11, 1929, entry is located at the end of the 1929 calendar year under "Memoranda":] In library to-night George Kelly & Dan Long Newman came in without ties & Mrs. Johnson, the librarian, made them go out & they came back in with great big ribbon ties & got everyone tickled. Mrs. J. got so mad but couldn't do a thing. [Dan Long Newman, age about twenty, was a son of Dr. John U. Newman, professor of Greek and Biblical studies at Elon College and the senior member on the faculty in 1929. Dan's sister Lila Newman taught fine arts at Elon College. His brother Joseph was a dentist in town. According to the 1930 census, Dan Long Newman was a public school teacher living at his father's residence. George D. Kelly was a junior from Durham, North Carolina; John Lowry was a sophomore from Peachland, North Carolina; Mrs. C.C. Johnson was an assistant librarian at Elon College.[163]]

April 12

Had lab this afternoon. Went to a Gypsy camp at MoonElon & had my fortune told. The girl's name was Margret Western & she was so cute. She promised to write to me & tell Jack C. [his] fortune like I wanted her to.

April 13 Saturday

Had ball game to-day with Wofford, S.C. We won 5–0. Met Carl Gibbon. Went with Andrews. Went to show here to-night. "Old Ironsides." Vada left me. "Let her go." [Wofford is a small liberal arts college located in Spartanburg, South Carolina. *Old Ironsides*, a silent film released in 1926 by Paramount Famous Lasky Corporation, is a historical drama starring Wallace Berry and George Bancroft. "Andrews" was probably Twiman Glenn Andrews (see entry for January 14, 1929).[164]]

April 14

Cut church. Wrote Jim Comer. Met Earl Register & Emmett Chandler from Durham while Slack & I were hunting four-leaf clovers on backside of campus & they came around & talked to us. [Jim Comer played on the

Seagrove High School basketball team during the 1927–28 season. He now was married and lived in High Point.]

April 15
Got letter from Howard. Hobert and Carl Register. Went to society. Still mad at V. [Vada Graves.]

April 16
Had freshman-sophmore debate to-night. Evelyn R., Aeta Dide, R. Richardson & H. Truitt (freshmen). Went to social hour & auditorium with John Lowry. [Evelyn Byrd Richardson was from Waverly, Virginia; Roy A. Richardson was from Suffolk, Virginia. On John Lowry, see entry for April 11, 1929.[165]]

April 17
Went to Religious Education building to-night. A big crowd was up there. Then went with "Lefty" Briggs to their commencement entertainment. I am seventeen to-day.

April 18
Wouldn't give John a date to-night because I had to study for biology test. Won a ball game with Wake Forest to-day. [Probably John Lowry.]

April 19
Had biology test this morning. Mr. Wasner played a guitar & ukulele and sang in chapel.

April 20 Saturday
Went home this morning. Mamma & Mabel went to High Point. Listened to radio to-night. Aunt Hattie came. Elon glee club sang over radio at Raleigh.

April 21
Went to birthday dinner at Wyatt Trogdon's to-day & played down at river. Came by B. Lucas's fish pond. Bood brought Howard & I back & we came by Chapel Hill. Saw all boys & met a Philippine boy. [The Bethel Lucas fishpond was located about two miles south of Auman's Crossroads. Wyatt Trogdon lived on a farm in the Auman's Crossroads community on the banks of the Little River.[166]]

April 22
Went down town & got my twenty dollar gold piece changed. Ate the box of things I brought from home. Wrote a short story to-night on "Out Where the West Begins."

April 23
Made up lab this afternoon. Oratorical contest of juniors began to-night. Wrote John Crowell a letter yesterday.

April 24
Wrote Jim a letter. Finished copying my short story. Went to chapel to hear junior orations. Came back with Grandpa Thompson. Prof. Powell is so interesting in Biology. [Probably Jim Comer.]

April 25
Planned to go home for [Seagrove High School] commencement day. Went with John to chapel to hear orations. Stood at the door with Dan Long Newman. [Probably John Lowry.]

April 26
Had last lab. to-day. Studied incubated egg. Prof. Powell lectured on evolution this morning. He is so good.

April 27 Saturday
Had ball game this afternoon with High Point. Beat them 8–2. Talked to Roland Smith & Hartly in Alamance [Hall] this afternoon. Went to show "Speed Classic" to-night. [*Speed Classic* is a silent melodrama released in 1928 by First Division Pictures starring Rex Lease and Mitchell Lewis. Ruth Roland Smith was a freshman from Siler City, North Carolina; Harold Waldo Hartly was a freshman from Homestead, Pennsylvania.[167]]

April 28
Rained awful hard this morning when we were at church. Lane R. & Preston Wright from Yancyville came to-day. Miss O'Quinn & Leta Auman also. Wrote another short story. [Leta Auman (1902–89), Mary's second cousin, was a sister of Alberta Auman, a freshman at Elon College.]

April 29 .
Today is the first time the Australian Ballot system has been used in this school to elect officers. Hiked in gym toward Burlington. Heard ball player orations to-night. They acted so funny. [The Australian ballot system allows people to cast votes namelessly to decide the outcome of an election.]

April 30
Went to ball game with Bob McLeod from Florida. Catawba won 4–1. Yesterday the spring football players had their game. To-night the glee club gave program.

May 1929

May 1
Went to Burlington this afternoon with Vada & Mildred. Got a pillow with "The House by the Side of the Road" written on it. [A poem by Sam Walter Foss (1858–1911).[168]]

May 2
Got ready to go home. Had date to-night with John Lowry. [On John Lowry, see entry for April 11, 1929.]

May 3
Went home this afternoon. Met Ivey & Aunt Belle in Greensboro. Went to recital there to-night. [Ivey Luck and Belle Cornelison were siblings.]

May 4 Saturday
Went to Pilot Mt. to-day on picnic with 9th grade and several others. Fred took his truck & Miss Spence. I went with Raeford Williams & we sat on back of truck. Had a big time. [Pearle Spence, age about twenty-two, taught music at Seagrove School. She was a daughter of J. Ed Spence, merchant in Coleridge Township. Mary is referring here to the ninth grade class at Seagrove School and to Fred Auman.[169]]

May 5
Went to Sunday school this morning. Heard commencement this afternoon & saw all seniors. Grandpa's folks came. Came back [to Elon] to-night with Gilmer [Auman] & Reese [Richardson]. [Mary is probably referring here to the commencement exercises at Seagrove High School.]

May 6
Went on field trip this afternoon to Shayes pond. Rained all time. Went with (Al) Fred Smith in Elizabeth Story's car. Had lots of fun. Crowded up. Went to Society to-night.

May 7
Last ball game this year with Bridgewater & beat them 19–0. Howard Allen gave me a check for "love." [Bridgewater is a denominational college affiliated with the Church of the Brethren located in the Shenandoah Valley of Virginia.]

May 8
Commencement day at home. Called us down in gym to-night & searched our rooms for stolen pin of Elizabeth's. Found it in Louise Hough's room.

[Perhaps the commencement exercises mentioned in the entry on May 5 were a rehearsal for today's activities.]

May 9
Socialized with "Lefty" Briggs to-night. Daddy came this morning.

May 10
Worked on my chart in Biology "Interrelationship of Organisms." Edith Lockey & Lucy Bone gave their recital to-night. [On Edith Lockey, see entry for March 18, 1929. Lucy Ione Boone was a senior from Burlington, North Carolina.[170]]

May 11 Saturday
Had English test this morning. Watched Prof. Guillet & Leota play tennis. Vada & I spent the night with Leota & Dolphine Irby at the hall. Ate sandwiches & strawberries & had lemonade. [Dolphine Aleathea Irby was a freshman from Enfield, North Carolina.[171]]

May 12
Mother's Day. Had the biggest time. Mattie, Julie Mae, V. & I all cut up & made out like we had some films in our Kodak & took everybody's picture. Met a boy from Wash. D.C. & talked to him with M. Caviness. Took pictures with Axpe. [Axpe was a student from Cuba. (See entry for January 8, 1929.) Merrill Louise Caviness was a junior from Portsmouth, Virginia.[172]]

May 13
Went to Burlington to-day & got a pair of white slippers.

May 14
Prof. Guillet gave me a French book as being one of his best students.

May 15
Paul Magee & Ella Marie Keyser gave a certificate recital to-night. [Ella Marie Keyser was a junior from Elon College, North Carolina.[173]]

May 16
Y.W.C.A. went on picnic. I had such a sore toe [so] I couldn't go.

May 17
Prof. Guillet took us on a picnic to Moonelon. Roasted wieners & went boat riding. Got letter from Momma. Choral Society gave "The Village Blacksmith." Benjamin DeLoacht, great singer was so good looking here.

May 18 Saturday
Last day of school before exams. Went to show to-night [and saw] Richard Dix in "Sporting Goods." [A 1928 comedy released by Paramount Famous Lasky Corporation.[174]]

May 19
Cut church. Talked to Andy this afternoon. Had a picture taken under the roses at the gate. Talked to Roland & Dan Long to-night on the steps & had them to write in my annual.

May 20
Took first exam to-day on Education. Rained all day. Studied Biology.

May 21
Had Biology exam this morning. Studied this afternoon. Fred Caddell & some boys planned to take Lib Davis home. Got people to write in my annual. [Fred Caddell, senior at Elon College, lived near the campus with his parents. His father, Hitta H. Caddell, was a medical doctor.[175]]

May 22
Had Bible & English exams to-day. Felt so relieved this afternoon after they were over. After lights went out we sang, moved trunks & cut up.

May 23
Packed my trunk this morning. Went down town several times. Lots of people are beginning to leave. Boys made an old car & put [it] in front of dormitory.

May 24
Played tennis early this morning. Went down town & to the [train] station. Went to Burlington this afternoon without a chaperon & met Carl Smith. He came over here to-night. Had a party in the Y.M.C.A.

May 25 Saturday
Went down town early this morning.

May 26
Talked to "Lefty" & Fred Caddell. Fred & I talked to-night. Didn't go to church & Miss Chandler made us come in. [On Gertrude Chandler, a housekeeper at Elon College, see entry for January 19, 1929.]

May 27
Went down town & went with Fred to get a speech from Ella Marie Keyser. Class day exercise this morning—came home [to Seagrove] this afternoon & it was pouring rain.

May 28
Went to see Harriet's children. Jean says she is my girl. Dorothy is so cute. Played with Wade. [Gene King was about three, Dorothy one. On the Elsie and Harriet King family, see entry for February 25, 1928. On Wade Harris, now about thirteen, see entry for March 25, 1928.]

May 29
Went to High Point to-day & got new music. "Wedding Bells are Breaking Up That Old Gang Of Mine." "Neapolitan Night." "Blue Hawaii." "Carolina Moon."

May 30
Got letter from Merrill Caviness at Washington D.C. Chappy wants my picture & wants to write to me. [On Merrill Caviness, see entry for May 12, 1929.]

May 31
Mrs. Harris is sick. Wrote Howard Allen, John Creel & Merrill Caviness.

June 1929

June 1 Saturday
Helped Wade wash dishes & get dinner. Made ice cream in Kelvinator. Went to High Point & got a silk voile dress. [Kelvinator was a brand of refrigerator sold at the time.]

June 2
Went to Sunday school. Ate dinner & went down to Wades. Ate ice cream. Daddy let Mabel & I drive Ford. Went to see Lillian & Alberta to-night.

June 3
Started reading "The Flat Tire" in Daily paper. Got a letter from Fred Caddell. Lillian & Alberta came to see me to-night. [*The Flat Tire* was a serialized version of Alma Sioux Scarberry's 1930 novel by the same title that was appearing in the *Greensboro Daily News*. See page four of the June 3, 1929, issue of the newspaper for an example.]

June 4
Went to Mrs. Comer & had her to make me a silk voile dress. Vada came to see me. Frank Leach came home from school to-day. [Frank Leach, a student at the state school for the deaf and dumb, is coming to Seagrove to spend the

summer with his parents. On the Leach family, see the entries for June 7 and December 22, 1928.]

June 5
John Crowell came to-night & we went to ride. He is leaving for Baltimore to-morrow. Howard came home from Carolina.

June 6
Ronie Boon, Wade, Lexie, Mabel & I played ball on the road late this evening. Went to Harriet's to-night & played with Jean. Played Howard's portable lots. [Wade Harris, Harriet and Gene King. Lexie Boon, age about twenty, was the son of Jason and Zeller Boon, farmers.[176]]

June 7
Somebody broke in Uncle David's store at 1:00 o'clock this morning. Everybody got up & got officers from Asheboro & bloodhounds & hunted them. [*The Courier* did not report this incident.]

Image 53: Mattie Luck's graduating class of 1908, Why Not Academy. The following year, she married Frank Auman.

June 8 Saturday
Went up to Mrs. Comer's. Came by Daddy's office. [This is probably a reference to Cora Comer, wife of James R. Comer Sr. See entry for February 23, 1928.]

June 9
Went to church. Came home and ate cake & ice cream. Rained all day. Went to Wade's—

June 10
Went to Asheboro to-night with Howard, Mabel & Boode & saw "The Singing Fool." [This is the second time Mary records seeing *The Singing Fool.* See entry for October 29, 1928.]

June 11
Thought I was going to Charlotte but it was Shiloh. Ha. Ha.!

June 12
Been riding Wade's bicycle. Played bridge & rook. [Bridge, a card game, became popular in the United States in the 1890s. It derives from whist, a much older card game. In 1925, Harold Sterling Vanderbilt introduced contract bridge, a modern version of the game. Mary, Mabel, and Howard became lifelong enthusiasts of playing contract bridge.[177]]

June 13 Saturday
So hot today. Went down town & came back & played rook with Mabel & Wade. Took Harriet some "Buccaneers." Went to work to-night.

June 14
Wade got letter from Carl & Herbert. Winfred Hoyle wrote me. [Margaret Winfred Hoyle was a freshman from Newton, North Carolina. Carl and Herbert Peters, ages about sixteen and fourteen respectively, were nephews of Mrs. A.C. Harris, Mary's neighbor in Seagrove. On the Harris and Peters families, see entries for March 25 and May 2, 1928.[178]]

June 15 Saturday
Rained all day. Went to Harriot's and played with Dorothy. Got a letter from Merrill [Caviness] saying that Chappy wanted to call me up.

June 16
Got letter from Fred. Said he might come to-day. Fred & Alberta came this afternoon. Went to ride with Wade, Howard & Mabel & saw wreck. Went to Why Not. Went to birthday dinner at N. King's. [Noah King. It is unclear whether Mary is referring to Fred Auman or Fred Caddell, or both.]

June 17
Euclid Auman started painting our house this morning. Went to High Point & looked at Parlor suite. [On Euclid Auman, see entry for June 20, 1928.]

June 18
Wade & I rode bicycles to schoolhouse. Went to Daddy's office & he made us a key.

June 19
Wrote Fred, Merrill, Winfred Hoyle & Mr. Cannon. Our blue hydrangea is so pretty. [Probably Fred Caddell and Merrill Caviness. C.M. Cannon was the registrar at Elon College.[179]]

June 20
Cooked & fixed lunch to take on trip to-morrow. Went over to see Alberta & Leta. [Leta Auman.]

June 21
Left home early this morning in Fred's truck with house on it. Rode all day. Camped near Blowing Rock. Scared so bad we didn't sleep much. [Blowing Rock is a resort town located in the Blue Ridge Mountains of northwestern North Carolina. Unfortunately, Mary does not make clear Fred's identity, but he was probably Fred Auman. See May 4, 1929, entry.]

June 22 Saturday
Left Blowing Rock this morning & came on to Asheville & then to Chimney Rock. Scenery is so pretty here. Camped on Lake Lure. [Asheville is the largest city in the mountains of western North Carolina; it is about one hundred and fifty miles west of Seagrove. Chimney Rock and Lake Lure are small vacation mountain communities located southeast of Asheville.]

June 23
Left Lake Lure early this morning & came back by Forest City, Charlotte & Albemarle. Saw Daddy & folks at Badin. Wade, Lillian, Lane & Joe went up there to-day. [Baden, a popular destination for picnickers and boaters, is a small town located on the shores of Badin Lake in Stanly County. It is about twenty-five miles west of Seagrove. Mary had an aunt and four first cousins living in Badin. They were the wife and children of her Uncle Everett Luck, a son of Charlie and Mary Luck. For more information on the Everett Luck family, see entry for July 16, 1929.]

June 24
Found out that Vada, Lane, Lillian & Joe went to Asheville too yesterday.

June 25
Grandma [Fannie Luck], Aunt Hattie & Mabel Davies came this afternoon. Got letter from Fred. [Mary is probably referring to Fred Caddell at Elon College.]

June 26
Wrote Fred. Got letter from Edith & she wants me to spend the fourth with her. [Either Edith McDowell or Edith Brower in Asheboro.]

June 27
[No entry.]

June 28
Went to High Point to-day with Daddy.

June 29 Saturday
Went to Star with Jim Comer & Lacy Harper to see Maxine & Ila Holt.

June 30
I drove to Jackson Springs to-day. Went to Dora Pattersons & had lots of fun with the boys & some [people] from Florida. [Dora Patterson (1877–1951), Mary's first cousin, was a daughter of Jason Auman (1850–1923). Dora was married to John Edward Patterson and had seven children. In 1930, she was living with her husband and two sons in Sand Hill Township, Moore County.[180]]

July 1929

July 1
Talmadge Brown, John Ward & Edith came down [from Asheboro] to-night but I was at Noah King's. [Either Edith McDowell or Edith Brower.]

July 2
Wrote to Fred. [Mary is probably referring to Fred Caddell.]

Image 54: Fourth of July Parade, 1920, Sunset Avenue, Asheboro, North Carolina.

July 3

Got letter from Cannon that I could get room no 38. [C.M. Cannon was the registrar at Elon College. See entry for June 19, 1929.]

July 4

Went to Asheboro. Rode in parade with Talmadge Brown. Went to ride with him & John Ward & to show. Went to dance to-night & to midnight show with George Ward & Tom [Bowman]. Stayed night with Edith. [Mary is referring here to the annual Asheboro Fourth of July celebration, which included a morning parade, afternoon prizefighter boxing matches in the city center, a dance at night, and a midnight movie at the Capitol Theater. Mayor C.C. Cranford, the town board, the local military company, local fire trucks, and the Asheboro Band headed the parade. Floats, mostly by businesses and social organizations, made up the bulk of the pageant. Mary rode in Talmadge Brown's car in the individual automobile part of the procession. After the parade, there were contests such as foot races, wheelbarrow races, three-legged races, and greasy pole climbing. An airplane flew overhead throughout the day featuring stunts and parachute jumping. Talmadge Brown, age about nineteen, was a son of I.T. Brown, U.S. Marshall, who lived in Asheboro. The 1930 U.S. Census lists Talmadge Brown as working in the parts department of a garage. George and John Ward, ages about eighteen and sixteen respectively, were the sons of Wiley L. Ward, treasurer at a cotton mill in Asheboro.[181]]

Image 55: Helen and Betsy Luck with Mabel and Mary Auman, about 1927.

July 5
George Ward & Tom Bowman came after dinner. Talmadge & John were aiming to take us home. Went to ride with John [Ward]. They all came by late to-night. [Tom Bowman, age about fifteen, was a son of Cephas and Ella Bowman of Asheboro. Cephas was a deputy tax collector and Ella was a salesclerk in a dry-goods store.[182]]

July 6 Saturday
At work on our porch. Carl & Herbert Peters are at Wade's. We went down there.

July 7
George & Tom came down to-night. Mamma & daddy went to Winston Salem to see Aunt Hattie. [Probably George Ward and Tom Bowman of Asheboro.]

July 8
Went to Jethro Almond's show here to-night. [Jethro Almond (1868–1959), a native of Stanley County, North Carolina, was a pioneer showman who owned and operated a circus in the early twentieth century.[183]]

July 9
George came to-night. On his way to S.C. Went to the show here. Jethro gave Mabel & I complementary tickets. [Probably George Ward.]

July 10
Went to Harris's to-night. Played rook and games. I was vaccinated for typhoid fever.

July 11
George came down to-night. I went to the show with Mrs. Harris. Got letter from George at noon & wrote him this afternoon.

July 12
Got letter from Fred. Got ukulele and practiced playing it & [incomplete]

July 13 Saturday
Went to Harris's to-night. They went to ride & left us kids there. Hahn Moore rode off with some man. [Hahn Moore, age about eighteen, was the daughter of Jefferson and Sallie Moore. Jefferson Moore was a grocery retailer in Seagrove.[184]]

Image 56: Captain Everett Luck (*center*), Company K, 120th
Infantry Regiment, 30th Division, France, 1918.

July 14
Meeting started here to-day. After church, George came & we went to ride. He
is 19 to-day. [A week of special religious services began today at the Seagrove
Christian Church. Services would be at 3:00 and 8:00 PM daily.[185]]

July 15
Went to church. Went to Asheboro & talked to Althea Presnell. [Althea
Presnell, age about nineteen, was the daughter of Walter and Hossie Presnell.
Walter Presnell was a horse and mule dealer in Asheboro. In January 1928,
Althea Presnell was a student at High Point College; in 1930, she was living
in Manhattan working for a telephone company.[186]]

July 16
Ivey & Aunt Belle went after Helen & Betsy. Went to church this afternoon & night. [Helen and Betsy Luck, Mary's first cousins, ages about twelve and thirteen, lived in Badin, North Carolina, with their mother, Jeanette, and their maternal grandparents, Robert and Mattie Dickens. (Robert Dickens owned a grocery store in Baden.) Their parents had separated. Their father, Everett Luck (born about 1893), was living in San Bernardino, California, where he would become an automobile sales representative. An experienced auto mechanic, Captain Everett Luck served in the U.S. Army in France in the nascent Army Motor Pool, 1918–19. After the battle of Bellicourt (September 29, 1918), Captain Luck was put in command of Company K, 120th Infantry Regiment, 30th Division, for several weeks. (Company K, composed mostly of men from Randolph County, North Carolina, suffered more than 50 percent casualties at Bellicourt, where they took part in an assault that broke through the Hindenburg Line.) By January 1919, he was commander of two Army Motor Transport Companies in France. In 1916–17, he had taken part in the Punitive Expedition against Pancho Villa while based at Camp Stewart, a U.S. Army encampment near El Paso, Texas.[187]]

July 17
Betsy & I played hooky. Didn't go to church. Got letter from John Crowell.

July 18
Helen & Betsy came out here this morning.

July 19
Drove the car to the schoolhouse and around yard. Meeting closed to-night. Uncle David & Mr. Cumings swapped cars. [The meeting to which Mary refers was the last of six days of special services held at the Christian Church. Reverend J.C. Cummings, a pastor from Hemp, probably led or assisted with the services. See entries for March 11, 1928, and July 14, 1929.]

July 20 Saturday
Went to High Point this morning. Drove car around in yard with Betsy [Luck] & Obeira [Leach].

July 21
Rained all day. Carl, Herb. & Wade came over & we played music & cut up—went to ride. I practiced driving. Went down to Harris's to-night. [Carl and Herbert Peters; Wade Harris.]

July 22
Looked for George to-night. Betsy [Luck] & I danced. [Mary is probably referring to George Ward of Asheboro.]

July 23
Played croquet with the boys.

July 24
Went with Helen & Betsy & Wades folk's to Badin. Went in bathing. Had lunch & saw Janet & Mrs. Dickens. [Helen and Betsy Luck, their mother Janet, and their grandmother, Mattie Dickens.]

July 25
Vaccinated to-day for typhoid. Drove car.

July 26
Uncle David, Aunt B—Helen & Betsy left early this morning for Langley Field. Wrote Fred & John. Went to ride with George. [Probably Fred Caddell, John Crowell, and George Ward.]

July 27 Saturday
Stayed with Ivey in store. Went to Wade's to-night. Told Carl & Herbie goodby.

July 28
Carl & Herb. went home to-day. Went to Grandpa's this morning. Drove Ivey's car. Went to ride ~~this~~ to-night with Dal Rich—Asheboro. T—Jim— [Words illegible.] [Dallas Rich, age about twenty, was the son of Elmer and Hattie Rich of Asheboro. Elmer Rich was a manufacturer of bricks. He provided the bricks for the construction of the Seagrove Hardware in 1915. Carl and Herbert Peters lived in Appalachia, Virginia. On the Peters family, see entry for May 2, 1928.[188]]

July 29
Took Alberta to ride & went to see Martha. She is talking of studying nursing at Johns Hopkins. [These are likely Alberta Auman and Martha Graves.]

July 30
Aunt Belle & the girls came back from Aunt Bertha's [at Langley Field, Virginia]. ["The girls" were Helen and Betsy Luck.]

July 31
Drove car to Grandpa's & we all went in swimming. [They went swimming at the "cat fish hole" in the Little River near Charlie Luck's house. See entry for January 15, 1928.]

Image 57: Seagrove Hardware in 2007; built in 1915.

August 1929

August 1
Betsy taught me the "toddle." Ruth & Annie Gean came down. [The "Toddle" was a dance that first appeared in 1917 and was popular among collegiate and flapper circles into the 1920s.[189]]

August 2
George & crowd of boys passed this morning going to Myrtle Beach. Mabel & I went with Daddy to Thomasville & High Point. [Mary was probably referring to George Ward of Asheboro.]

August 3 Saturday
Betsy & I danced. Got new parlor suite. Got letter from Fred. He is coming Sunday.

August 4
Helen & Betsy went home [to Badin]. Edith Mc. came this aft. & spent night with me. Went to ride to-night with Jones & Poole from Chatham, Va. Got card from George. [Edith McDowell of Asheboro. The card probably came from George Ward at Myrtle Beach.]

August 5
Edith & I went riding this morning with Jones & Pool. Took her home this aft. Played croquet & saw George pass coming home. [This was probably George Ward coming home from Myrtle Beach. See entry for August 2, 1929.]

August 6
George came for a few minutes this aft.

August 7
Got letter from Fred saying that he might come Sunday. [This is probably a reference to Fred Caddell.]

August 8
[No entry.]

August 9
Went to ride several times. Played croquet. Mary Lee & I cleaned & decorated the parlor.

August 10 Saturday
Helen & Betsy & Genette came to-day. Howard, Ivey & Ben Auman left to-night for New York & Atlantic City. ["Genette" was likely Helen and Betsy's mother, Jeanette Luck. See entry for July 16, 1929.]

August 11
John Crowell came to-night. Went to ride. He's going to State College to study agriculture.

August 12
Got card from Howard. [Howard Auman in New York or Atlantic City. See entry for August 10, 1929.]

August 13
John Crowell came to-night. Went to ride.

August 14
Drove car to Uncle Alf's to get beans. Rode horses. [Mary's paternal grandfather, Franklin Auman, died in 1911. Franklin's son, Alpheus Auman (1880–1959), whom Mary refers to here as "Uncle Alf," inherited the family farm, which was located about four miles west of Seagrove in the Auman's Crossroads community at the intersection of the Burney Road and the Mountain Road (today North Carolina highway 134). On Alpheus Auman's exhibits at the Randolph County Fair in 1928 and 1929, see entries for September 29, 1928 and October 19, 1929.]

Image 58: Alpheus Auman house at Auman's Crossroads about 1980 (built about 1915 on the site of the Franklin Auman (1826–1911) house).

August 15
Left at 3:30 this morning for Aunt Bertha's at Langley Field. Went via Chapel Hill, Suffolk, James River Bridge. Got there about 12:00.

August 16
Drove car around house. Flirted with one of the boys. Raced with a boy on motorcycle.

August 17 Saturday
Went to Ocean View & Norfolk to-day by ferry. Met Richard More [a] boy from York, Pennsylvania. Walked with the kids across the bridge. ["The kids" were the children of Lebbeus and Bertha Auman—Sam, Thomas, and Evelyn. Mary may have been referring to Richard D. Moore, age about thirty, an electrical contractor from Hanover, Pennsylvania, where he lived with his sister and brother-in-law in 1930.[190]]

August 18
Talked to Moore this aft. Walked across bridge & talked to guard. Went to Fort Monroe & Buckroe Beach to dance.

August 19
Left early this morning [for home]. Came back by Raleigh.

August 20
Went to see Alberta & Mildred.

August 21
Looked for George. [Probably George Ward of Asheboro.]

August 22
Someone passed and hollered at me about eight to-night. I wonder! [The front of the Frank Auman house at Seagrove is about ten yards back from Old Highway 70—today State Highway 705.]

August 23
Played rook with Wade & Mabel.

August 24 Saturday
Spent day in High Point shopping. Got brown dress, hat & slippers.

August 25
Went to Association to-day at Cottons Creek. Met Griffin, Ray Galimore & went to ride with Ralph B. Drove Bood's car & met John Ward.

August 26
Mabel, Alberta, Mildred & I went to ride this afternoon.

August 27
Wrote Fred this morning.

August 28
Got new records. "Pagan Love Song," "Weary River," "Happiness Lane."

August 29
Looked for George. Howard got new record. "Wedding of the Painted Doll."

August 30
Went to High Point shopping to-day.

August 31 Saturday
Boodie, Mabel & I went to Asheboro to show to-night.

Chapter 4

Elon College Days—The Second Year

In her first academic year at Elon College, Mary wrote in her diary about breaking the rules on smoking, dancing, leaving campus, and dating without permission. Nevertheless, the number of infringements was small and without consequence. Apparently, school authorities did not know of her violations. She did note that several of her friends were caught and either "campused" or "probated" as punishment.

During the 1920s—the Age of Jazz, the automobile, the flapper, and prohibition—social mores and gender roles were rapidly changing in America. The Elon College restrictions on dating and casual socialization with members of the opposite sex were throwbacks rooted in puritanical and Victorian values that began to lose currency with the advent of urbanization, industrialization, and the changes brought about by the catastrophe of World War I. Women were now voting, driving automobiles, going to college, and working outside the home in occupations formerly restricted to men. During Mary's tenure at Elon College, students, male and female, rebelled against the social restrictions forced on them by school authorities. This was particularly true for the female students. Times were changing—especially views about the proper conduct of young women in society. Mary and her rebellious female classmates were harbingers of the changes that would take place in the role young women played in society in the future, especially during the 1960s. In that light, one can now view them as proto-feminists.

As the months went by in her second year at Elon College, Mary became ever more rebellious against the social boundaries imposed on her. While in high school, Mary had freely associated with male classmates and had occasionally gone on dates with them. In the summers and on weekends when she went home from college, she dated boyfriends, including going to movies, to parties, and on rides in cars with them. On occasion, she took car trips with friends—sometimes driving the family automobile herself—to distant towns such as Pinehurst, West End, Asheboro, Asheville, High Point, and Greensboro. When she returned to Elon College after a weekend or a summer at home, gender regulations imposed by college authorities required her to accept social restrictions that seemed unrealistic to her. Little wonder that she rebelled.

Despite the ban on dating, Mary managed to attract several male admirers—most of them star college athletes; she always seemed to be in love. She could meet with boys at certain locations on campus set aside for "socialization," which members of the college staff monitored. Occasionally she broke the ban on dating by clandestinely rendezvousing with a boyfriend somewhere in the dark corners of the campus. Alternately, she might meet up with him off campus during a trip to Burlington or during a visit to the small business district adjacent to the campus. Campus authorities charged Mary several times with violating the dating rules or leaving the campus without permission, and restricted her to campus for several days at a time. Once they put her on probation, a punishment meted out to students upon their fifth conviction by the executive board.[191]

September 1929

September 1
Went to Janie & Boyd King's. George & Talmadge came by. Drove to Grandpa's to-night. Alberta, Boyd & I went to ride. John came. [George Ward, Talmadge Brown, Alberta Auman, probably John Crowell. Janie and Boyd King, ages about thirty-two, lived in Seagrove. Boyd's occupation was in "milling" at a Cedar Mill. The Kings had two young children and five boarders living with them. Three of their boarders were public-school teachers.[192]]

September 2
Drove car over to see Alberta & Mildred.

September 3
Went to High Point this aft. Boodie, Mabel & I went to Asheboro to-night. I drove. Talked to Clarence Overman. [In 1930, a Clarence Overman, age nineteen, boarded at the house of Eugene Lewallen in Asheboro. The census listed Clarence as a "botteler" at the Coca Cola plant.[193]]

September 4
Clarence Overman called & came by to see me to-night. George called & came down & we went to ride. He is so sweet. Finished my pink evening dress.

Image 59: Ivey Luck's service station, café, and grocery store in 2007
(built around 1930 with additions later).

September 5
Came to Elon this morning with Alberta & Howard. Matriculated and saw everybody.

September 6
Met classes this morning. Taking Eng. II, French II, Psychology, Philosophy II, Biology II, Ed. II.

September 7 Saturday
Went to Burlington this aft. Saw "Wonder of Women." Had annual reception to-night. George, Wally, Fred, Kelly & I drank 5 glasses of punch. [*Wonder of Women* is a drama released by MGM in 1929 starring Lewis Stone and Leila Hyams.[194]]

September 8
Went to church—talked to "Charlie" this aft. & had so much fun. He introduced me to "Wagner" & I talked to him.

September 9
Wrote home & [to] Betsy. Talked to Fred. Got letter from John—went to Society. [Betsy Luck of Badin, Fred Caddell, probably John Crowell.]

September 10
Wrote Clarence Overman. Had date with Wagner to-night. Moved to room 32.

September 11
Wrote John. Went to see Lucy Crowell & Ruth Dogget. Cute freshmen girls. [Probably John Crowell. On Ruth Doggett, see entry for October 8, 1929.]

September 12
Went to Burlington & saw "Follies of 1929." Plenty good. Went to social hour with Dunn from Mt. Gilead. [*Fox Movietone Follies of 1929* is a musical comedy issued by Fox Film Corporation in 1929 starring John Breeden and Lola Lane. Edward Lacey Dunn was a freshman from Mt. Gilead, North Carolina.[195]]

September 13
Got letter from Mabel. Went to social hour & talked to Dan Long [Newman].

September 14 Saturday
Went down town this aft. Saw "The Air Circus" here to-night. Went down town after show & walked back with Dan. [*The Air Circus* is a drama released in 1928 by Fox Film Corporation starring Louise Dresser and David Rollins.[196]]

September 15
Cut church. Went down town this aft. Looked for Clarence O. Wrote George & daddy to-night. [Clarence Overman and George Ward of Asheboro.]

September 16
Lane Russell came to-night. Wagner made me mad in drugstore. Talked to Fred in book store.

September 17
Up before board for my first time for going down town Sat. night. Campused 2 days. Got letters from George & Clarence.

September 18
Wrote George this aft. Florra Page & I didn't go on Y.W. picnic. She went down town & got stuff to eat.

September 19
Got letter from Jim & pictures. Went down town. Ate lolly pops. [Probably Jim Comer, who at this time was living in High Point, North Carolina.]

September 20
Got letter & check from Daddy. He wrote me to take music & I want to take art. Some opposition! Eh?

Image 60: Fred Caddell, senior at Elon College, 1930.

September 21 Saturday
Went to show to-night. "The Speed Spook." Walked back with Fred & he gave me Sunday school cards. [*The Speed Spook* is a 1924 comedy-drama released by East Coast Films starring Johnny Hines and Faire Binney.[197]]

September 22
Cut church. Cold as heck all day & no heat. Howard & John came & talked to them during quiet hour. Looked for George but he did not choose to come. [Probably Howard Auman and George Ward, possibly John Crowell.]

September 23
Went to Society to-night. Wantel L. [Wantel Lambeth] & Adna Lane gave a play. Made a date to have my picture taken & looked at annuals.

September 24
Florra's people came Sunday & brought her lots of things to eat.

September 25
Fred & I went to the depot & weighed. 122 + 170 = 292.

September 26
Had pep meeting to-night. Walked with Fred [Caddell]. Got Fred's ring.

September 27
Mary Sue & I went down town to-night. Went to Burlington with Elsie & some girls & came back on bus.

September 28 Saturday
Played Catawba & beat. Came by new café. Had a bonfire and show to-night.

September 29
Cut church. Looked for George but he didn't come. [Probably George Ward of Asheboro.]

September 30
Got letter from John this aft. and morning. Went to new café. Rained all afternoon. [Probably John Crowell.]

October 1929

October 1
Pinkie played his guitar & sang in the drugstore. Got letter from George saying he took John to school. [George and John Ward of Asheboro.]

October 2
Studied to-night for tests.

October 3
Had Phil. test this morning—. Socialized with Fred this aft. in drugstore & to-night on walk and down town.

October 4
Played A.C.C. this aft & beat 40–0. Talked to Fred in café. Wrote John, George, Carl & Vada. Got letter from her this morning. [Possibly John Crowell, George Ward, Carl Peters. A.C.C. refers to Atlantic Christian College located in Wilson, North Carolina. In 1990, school authorities changed the name of this denominational institution to Barton College in honor of a founder of the Christian Church.[198]]

October 5 Saturday
Got letter from Howard wanting to go home this week-end.

October 6
Sapp & I went down town. Talked to Fred. Got letter from Clarence O. [Vera
Annette Sapp was a junior from Douglas, Georgia.[199]]

October 7
Went to Burlington with Louise, Elsie & Allie. Wrote cards back here.
[Probably Louise Hough.]

October 8
Talked to Fred some to-night. Ruth Dogget is going to move in with me. [Ruth Marie
Doggett was a freshman from Summerfield (Guilford County), North Carolina. In
1930, she was living with her mother, Lula Doggett. Her father, Thomas Doggett
(born about 1860), probably deceased in 1930, had been a farmer.[200]]

October 9
Pie Kappa Taus are begging me to join their sororities—everybody is playing
with "Yo-Yo's."

October 10
Talked to Dick Caddell to-night. Dean saw us down town. Roland Smith
gave me his complimentary ticket to game. ["Dean" is a reference to Louise
Savage, dean of women. On Dean Savage, see entry for November 16, 1928.
On Roland Smith, see entry for January 28, 1929.]

October 11
Had biggest time at game at Wake Forest. Greshon met me & brought me
sandwiches. John came by. [Possibly John Crowell. Julius Carl Gresham was
a senior from Beuloville, North Carolina.[201]]

October 12 Saturday
Went on special bus to Wake Forest game. We lost 26–6 yesterday. To-night
—went to show & had date with Gresham but Fred took his place.

October 13
Had such a good time after dinner. Everybody got to pulling hair & ties and
playing on campus—Dean [Savage] made us stop. Talked to Fred to-night in
front of Alamance [Hall] instead of going to church.

October 14
Went to Burlington this afternoon & saw John Gilbert in "His Glorious
Night." Belle chaperoned & we came by down town to-night & I met Fred.
[*His Glorious Night* is a romance released by MGM in 1929 starring John
Gilbert and Catherine Dale Owen.[202]]

October 15
Up before board to-night and campused four days for being down town Friday night. Ruth Dogget is going to move in with me Friday. [On Ruth Doggett, see entry for October 8, 1929.]

Image 61: Ruth Doggett, Mary's roommate in the fall of 1929.

October 16
O'Kelly Monument unveiled here this morning & got my pictures back. [Reverend James O'Kelly led a group of dissenters in Virginia and North Carolina who in 1794 seceded from the Methodist Church to form the Christian Church.[203]]

October 17
Had French test this morning. Had pep meeting to-night. Thought about joining Pi Kappa Tau Society but decided not to—[Pi Kappa Tau was a sorority on the Elon College campus in 1929.]

October 18
Socialized with Fred on walk to-night. New mom & Dean Savage [are] sick. Had pep meeting & Roland read telegram from High Point [College] saying we were yellow bums.

October 19 Saturday
Alberta & I left on 11:30 bus. Got home & went to fair with Daddy, Betsy, Helen & Mabel to-night. Beat High Point 14–7 this afternoon. [The Randolph County Fair ran from Tuesday to Saturday. It was estimated that about ten thousand people attended the fair Tuesday night—the largest crowd ever at the fair. Mary's Uncle Alpheus Auman, as last year, presented an "individual farm exhibit." Two of his sons, Noah and Arthur, ages fourteen and seventeen respectively, assisted him in this endeavor.[204]]

October 20
Went with Ivey to Grandpa's this morning. Went to ride with George this aft. & he gave me a grand picture [of himself]. Mamma, Mabel & Daddy brought me back [to Elon]. [Mary is probably referring to George Ward.]

October 21
So homesick to-day. Hardly spoke to Fred (babe-y). Sent George my big picture.

October 22
Got letter from George. Said Talmadge & Edith were going to bring him up sometime.

October 23
Wantell Lambeth & I hiked to Gibsonville. We became thieves & robbed the 5 & 10 cent store. [Gibsonville is a small Guilford County town about two miles west of Elon College. Wantell Lambeth, age about eighteen, was a daughter of Hessa and Minnie Lambeth, merchants who owned a dry goods store in Elon College.[205]]

October 24
Carmelia & I hiked out toward Caddell's home & got leaves and decorated our rooms. [This is a reference to the home of Hitta Caddell, MD, father of Fred Caddell. On the Caddells, see entry for May 21, 1929.]

October 25
Modelle [Maedell] & I hiked to Gibsonville and met Howard Leslie & his roommate going home. Had lots of fun in drug store eating coconuts. [It is possible that Mary was referring to Howard *and* Leslie Auman in the first sentence. Maedell Lambeth, age about sixteen, was Wantell Lambeth's sister. For data on the Lambeth family, see entry for October 23, 1929.]

October 26 Saturday
Got letter from Carl. Went to show to-night "Prep & Pep." [A comedy-drama released by Fox Film Corporation in 1928 starring David Rollins and Nancy Drexel. Carl Peters of Appalachia, Virginia. See entry for May 2, 1928 for information on Carl Peters.[206]]

October 27
Spent afternoon with Modelle. Went to play here to-night. "Lar—." [Spelling unclear.] Wrote to Clarence. ["Modelle" is a reference to Maedell Lambeth. See entry for October 25, 1929. Probably Clarence Overman.]

October 28
Went to Society to-night. Paid no attention to "babe-y." [A reference to Fred Caddell. See entry for October 21, 1929.]

October 29
Rainy all day. Madelle came to see me. Ruth, Polly, Jeff & I went down town this afternoon & library to-night. Made out book report. [Maedell Lambeth, Ruth Doggett.]

October 30
Got letter from George & John. Worked in lab all afternoon & Fred studied in Lefty's room— [George Ward, John Crowell, Fred Caddell, Lefty Briggs. Mary made no mention of the stock market crash that panicked Wall Street the day before, known since as "Black Tuesday." As the months passed, she seemed oblivious to the growing economic depression. Mary had little reason for concern. Her family and the families of most of her relatives and friends endured the economic decline with minimal losses. Indeed, in the mid-1930s, during the heart of the Great Depression, her father and her Uncle Ivey Luck each built commodious new homes, her father in Asheboro, her uncle in Seagrove. Seagrove Lumber Company, Seagrove Hardware, Cornelison's Dry Goods Store, Ivey Luck's combined service station, grocery, and café, all survived the depression. In 1934, the stockholders of the Bank of Seagrove voluntarily voted to liquidate assets and close the bank; depositors were paid 100 percent.[207]]

October 31
Cut up & boiled cats this afternoon in lab. Halloween night & no fun. Talked to "Lefty" to-night. Went down town. Fred went to Burlington.

November 1929

November 1
Got letter from Mamma saying that Ben Bean had shot himself & his wife & that Mrs. Tom Monness [Maness] & Mrs. Tom Garner were dead. Went to Burlington & saw "On with the Show." [A musical issued by Warner Brothers Pictures in 1929 starring Betty Compson and Louise Fazenda.[208]]

November 2 Saturday
Went to ball game at Greensboro Stadium this aft. H.P [High Point College] beat us 13–6. Saw "Mother Machrie" here to-night. Mary Sue & I left.

[*Mother Machrie* is a melodrama released by Fox Film Corporation in 1928 starring Bette Bennett and Neil Hamilton.[209]]

November 3
Wrote Mamma & George [Ward]. John [Crowell] came a while this afternoon.

November 4
Talked to Estelle a while this afternoon. Initiated new members in society to-night—Like to laughed myself to death.

November 5
Had English & Physiology tests this morning.

November 6
Got letter from Mamma & George. Went down town twice to-night. Talked to Paul Wagner some—Mrs. Fab—[illegible name] made me leave library this morn.

November 7
Herbeil Gould sang here to-night.

November 8
After lab, I went with Ann Ruth Harding to meet bus & went home. Went to corn-shucking at Grandpa's to-night. [A "corn-shucking" was an American rural tradition in which farmers in a community would help each other in the labor-intensive work of shucking their corn crops of their husks. The receiver of the communal assistance, the host farmer, provided drinks, food, dancing, music, and other entertainments. Annie Ruth Harden was a junior from Graham, North Carolina.[210]]

November 9 Saturday
Went to Aunt Belles & to the store this morning. Went to church. George, Talmadge, Stauton P. & Tom B. came to-night & Edith B., Edith McD. & Lucile R. Thurman Cox got burned. [George Ward, Talmadge Brown, Tom Bowman, Edith Brower, Edith McDowell—all from Asheboro. Thinking that he was using kerosene, Thurman Cox inadvertently threw gasoline on some embers in a church stove to build a fire. The gasoline exploded, covering the top half of his body with flames, burning off his clothes. He died four days later. Thurman Cox, the son of William and Angie Cox, farmers, was a member of Seagrove High's 1927–28 basketball team.[211]]

November 10
Mabel & I made candy & went to the store & got me lots of things to bring back. I went to school this aft. Ivey & Mabel brought me back [to Elon] to-night.

November 11
Madelle came up & we went down town to-night. [Maedell Lambeth.]

November 12
Got Psychology paper back. I made the highest score. Got letter from George.

November 13
Thurman Cox died to-day. Started taking piano under Prof. Velie. Wrote George special delivery. [Probably George Ward of Asheboro. Mr. C. James Velie taught piano and organ; Mrs. Zenith Hurst Velie taught piano and voice. On Thurman Cox, see entry for November 9, 1929.[212]]

November 14
Went to Burlington & got black hat & silk wool dress. Francis & Vada got new long dresses.

November 15
Got letter from George this morning. Talked to boys from Emory & Henry [College] to-night. [Emory and Henry College, affiliated with the United Methodist Church, is located in the mountains of southwest Virginia.]

November 16 Saturday
Fred & I socialized until after the show to-night at the front gate.

November 17
Fred & I & Ruth & George stayed out during church to-night. Mrs. Edwards saw us go down town & followed us & we hid in alley. [Fred Caddell, probably Ruth Doggett, possibly George Ward. Miss Minnie Edwards was matron of girls' dormitory.[213]]

November 18
Some violinist was here to-night. I didn't go. Went down town with Alma Kimball. [Alma Eaton Kimball was a senior from Manson, North Carolina.[214]]

November 19
Went to Burlington and saw Illusions, Ruth & I. [*Illusions* is a 1929 silent movie made in France starring Pierre Batcheff and Gaston Jacquet and directed by Lucien Mayrargue.[215]]

November 20
Got letter from Howard saying he ~~might~~ would come by for me Thanksgiving.

November 21
Faculty gave a Womanless Wedding to-night. Polly & I hid from Mrs. Ed. in the ally & came in the front gate. ["Womanless Weddings"—comic presentations in which men acted the roles of all members of the wedding ceremony—have been widely used by schools, civic organizations, and churches as fundraisers. "Mrs. Ed." was probably a reference to Miss Minnie Edwards, matron of girls' dormitory at Elon College.[216]]

November 22
Got letter from Talmadge saying he may come Sunday. [This is probably Talmadge Brown of Asheboro.]

November 23 Saturday
Went to show with Madelle. Left & went down town. Renie & Polly gave us a party to-night. Talked to Fred in café & [incomplete entry]

November 24
Didn't go to church. Freshmen entertained us at S.S. Wrote letters. Sleet everywhere.

November 25
Belle & I went to Burlington & saw Clara Bow in "Saturday Night Kid." [A romantic comedy released by Paramount Famous Lasky Corporation in 1929 starring Clara Bow and James Hall.[217]]

November 26
Looking forward to going home.

November 27
Howard came by for me. Went to a wiener roast at Raeford W. He & a Callicut boy brought Mabel & I home. ["Raeford W" is a reference to Raeford Williams. See entry for January 10, 1928.]

November 28
Thanksgiving!! Drove Ford this aft. up to see Raeford. Had date with John Crowell to-night. George [Ward] came too & Grandma [Fannie Luck] came to-night.

November 29
Had date with Talmadge Brown to-night. Went to Greensboro to see "Two Black Crows." Freezing cold. ["Two Black Crows" is probably a reference to

two characters in the 1929 comedy-drama *Why Bring That Up?* released by Paramount Famous Lasky Corporation starring Charles E. Mack and George Moran. Greensboro is located about thirty-seven miles north of Seagrove.[218]]

November 30 Saturday
George came to-night. Mabel & I made candy & cakes & went to see Alberta & Mildred. Daddy killed me some birds.

Image 62: Howard Auman's bird dog Old Dan pointing
to a covey of quail, about 1930.

December 1929

December 1
Mabel & I made pictures & went to Aunt Belles this morning. Momma fixed me the best things to take back [to Elon College]. Mr. Auman brought [drove Mary and possibly others back to Elon College?]. Saw Fred & Maedell [illegible word].

December 2
Maedell spent the night with me. Sleeted & rained all morning.

December 3
Went to Burlington & got some woolen sox—blue, yellow & red.

December 4
Maedell brought me a lot of things to eat to-night.

December 5
Took the awfulest cold to-day.

December 6
Went to Burlington this afternoon. Bummed with Sapp & "Jeff." Rode in Jeff's car. Got box of candy from Mabel. [Mary violated college rules by hitchhiking and riding in a male's car without the Dean's authorization.]

December 7 Saturday
Went to show here to-night.

December 8
Looked for Talmadge. Maedell & I walked and went down town. I lost Anna O.['s] ring & we all hunted [for] it.

December 9
Went to studio with Wantell & down town.

December 10
Before the board to-night & campused 6 days. [It is possible that Mary was "campused 6 days" for riding in Jeff's car. (See entry for December 6, 1929.) Alternatively, perhaps it was for going to downtown Burlington without permission, or for both reasons.]

December 11
Went down town just five times to-day.

December 12
Studied Psy. with Lois in Delta U. room this aft. Wrote John & Howard. Maedell & I had lots of fun at the recital to-night. [Howard Auman, Maedell Lambeth, probably John Crowell.]

December 13
Fred & I talked a little while to-night. Studied Biol. with Edith Wright. [Sara Edith Wright was a junior from Asheboro, North Carolina.[219]]

December 14 Saturday
Got letter from Mamma saying that Aunt Margaret died yesterday. [Margaret Auman (née Martin, 1885–1929), wife of Alpheus Auman, was the mother of ten children.]

December 15
Studied all day. Went to see Wantell & Maedell.

December 16
Had Eng. test this morning. Studied this afternoon for Psy. exam tomorrow.

December 17
Had Psy. & Ed. exams to-day +

December 18
Had French & Biol. exams to-day—Socialized with Fred at gate & down town to-night.

December 19
Daddy came after me this morning. Went to Greensboro & shopped with Mamma.

December 20
Mabel, Alberta & Mildred & I went down rode & got Holly & Christmas tree. [Perhaps Mary meant to write "road" instead of "rode."]

December 21 Saturday
Decorated & fixed up parlor. Got electric lights for tree & red lights for room.

December 22
Went riding this afternoon in Ford. Snowed all day. Wade & I made snow cream.

December 23
Sleeted this morning on top of snow. Myrtle & Bertha came & stayed until Christmas. [Myrtle and Bertha, daughters of Alpheus and Margaret Auman, were Mary's first cousins. Their mother had died just nine days earlier. (See entry for December 14, 1929.) On Alpheus Auman, see entry for August 14, 1929.]

December 24
Jim Comer came to-night. Mabel & I went to Asheboro & got table for parlor. Mabel, H. [Howard] & I went to H.P. & got dress. [On Jim Comer, see entry for February 23, 1928.]

December 25
Shot fire-crackers down town with the boys. Daddy went fox hunting this morning. We all went to Grandpa's for dinner. Fred & Wantel came by. [Probably Fred Caddell and Wantell Lambeth from Elon College.]

Image 63: *From left*, Bertha, Beulah, and Myrtle, daughters of Alpheus
and Margaret Auman, about 1930.

December 26
Got picture & mesh bag from John Crowell. Worked in store & drove car.
[Mary's father owned a general store that was located across the highway from
the Seagrove Hardware.]

December 27
Had date with Clarence Overman to-night. He gave me a compact.

December 28 Saturday
Got letter from Mr. Cannon saying that he would not count my Biol grade.
[C.M. Cannon was the registrar at Elon College. See entry for June 19, 1929.]

December 29
Grandpa's folks came for dinner & Aunt Belle, Uncle D. [David] & Uncle
Jasper. Went to ride with R. B. & to Greensboro to-night with Tal. B. ["Tal. B."
is probably a reference to Talmadge Brown of Asheboro. Jasper Auman (1852–
1933) was a half-brother of Mary's father. Around 1918, he built a general store
adjacent to Frank Auman's store in Seagrove.]

Image 64: Jasper Auman, about 1910, owner of a General Merchandise Store in Seagrove, 1918 to about 1930.

December 30
Mabel started in school. I went down to see Mrs. Charles in café. I was leader at C.E. to-night. [On Mrs. Ross Charles, see entry for August 8, 1928.]

December 31
Took Mabel to school. Talked to Mrs. Charles & she told me about "Oh You Know." Wade, Mabel & I played & rode bicycles, ate onions & tomatoes.

January 1930

Image 65: Alpheus and Margaret Auman and children—*from left*, Gordon, Strawda, and Fred—about 1910.

January 1
Went to Uncle Alpheus's to-night & played with the kids. Drove car lots to-day. John called. [Probably John Crowell.]

January 2
Heard old man Henderson talk about chain stores to-night. Carried Mabel to school & rode lots. Howard went to school to-day.

January 3
Came back to school to-~~night~~ day. Alberta [Auman] drove part way & scared me so bad. Registered this aft. Mamma & I went to see Aunt Eis [spelling unclear] & Mr. Comer. [Probably James R. Comer Sr. of Seagrove. See entry for February 23, 1928.]

January 4 Saturday
Went to Ed. this morning. Went to Greensboro to see "The Vagabond Lover." Stayed with "Little Kip." Anne Va. came to see me to-night. [*The Vagabond Lover* is a 1929 RKO comedy-drama starring Rudy Vallee and Sally Blane. The identity of "Little Kip" is unknown. "Anne Va." is a reference to Anna Virginia Britt. See entry for November 29, 1928.[220]]

January 5
Went to church. Missed Sunday S. on account of my breakfast. Mabel sent my jacket.

January 6
Went to town & saw Joan Crawford in "Untamed." "Chant of Jungle" was theme song. [*Untamed* is a 1929 MGM comedy-drama-musical costarring Robert Montgomery.[221]]

January 7
Had ball game here to-night with High Point "Y" & won. ["Y" is short for Y.M.C.A.]

January 8
Painted my first picture in art to-day—a parrot on glass. Mabel sent me a box of candy.

January 9
Slipped off & went to Burlington to-day. Saw "Love, Live & Learn." I cried. Got a pair of slippers. [The editor cannot locate a record of a movie titled *Love, Live, and Learn*. Mary was probably referring to *Love, Live, and Laugh* released by Fox film Corporation in 1929 starring George Jessel and Lila Lee.[222]]

January 10
Started a new picture—a peacock on glass. [In time, Mary would become an accomplished amateur artist.]

January 11 Saturday
Dean [Savage] gave us a candy-pulling in the kitchen to-night.

January 12
Looked for Tal. Brown to-day. Talked to [Vera Annette] Sapp all aft. in infirmary. Didn't get bid. [Talmadge Brown of Asheboro. A "bid" is an invitation to join a sorority or some other group.]

January 13
Wrote Howard to come by for me Sat. to go home Fri. Planned to move up with Sapp. So down hearted. [There were at least three causes of Mary's depression: her recent split with her old friend and roommate Vada Graves; her failure on the previous day to get a bid to a sorority; her troubles with school authorities over her violations of college rules regulating off-campus activities of female students.]

January 14
Fred didn't even notice me to-night. Made up my mind to do differently from now on—went to studio & painted. Howard is nineteen.

January 15
Wrote Howard & got letter from Tal. saying he could come next Sun. Wrote Mrs. Charles. Wore Annie Ruth's short fur coat. [Mrs. Ross Charles was the owner of the café in Seagrove.]

January 16
Worked at studio all aft. Had music lesson this morning. Wrote Tal. Went down town with Wantell.

January 17
Howard came by for us. Awful cold (especially for rumble seat).

January 18 Saturday
Drove car down town [Seagrove]. Awful cold. Went to store & café to see Mrs. Charles.

Image 66: Girls Basketball Team, Seagrove High School, 1930,
Mabel Auman holding ball.

January 19
Went to Sunday school & to Aunt Belles. Came back [to Elon College] tonight. Played peg with Wade, Cecil & Beaufort. [Wade Harris, Cecil and Buford Leach.]

January 20
Went to studio but was too homesick to paint any.

January 21
So blue—had nothing to do with Fox.

January 22
Had date with Jimmie [Stewart] for ball game with H.P.C. [High Point College]. Went to Greensboro & saw Maurice Chevalier in "Love Parade." [A musical costarring Jeanette MacDonald issued by Paramount Famous Lasky Corporation in 1929. James Ellington Stewart was a sophomore from Greensboro, North Carolina.[223]]

January 23
Had date with Jimmie Stewart to-night. He's so cute.

January 24
Had date with Charlie Roberts to-night. Talked to Fred later & he got all right once more (for the present). [Charles Neil Roberts was a sophomore from Atlanta, Georgia.[224]]

January 25 Saturday
Went to see Sapp & we went down town. She's a real kid. I like her lots—Fred talked to me in drugstore— [On Vera Annette Sapp, see entry for October 6, 1929.]

January 26
Went to church. Stayed with Sapp & we carried on a lively conversation about—

January 27
Talked to Fred to-night at drugstore. Spent the night with Sapp.

January 28
Walked with Fred down town this morning. Worked in studio & talked to Kipka down town to-night. He gave me friendly advice. [Edward Eugene Kipka was a senior from Mooresville, North Carolina.[225]]

January 29
Fred left this morning on basketball tour. Didn't tell me goodbye.

January 30
Missed Fred. Planned to go home to-morrow. Snowed all night.

January 31
Left on 11:20 bus this morning & went home. Lucy waited with me till the bus came. Big snow. Talked to Mr. White— [Probably Harvey White, public school teacher at Seagrove School. See January 12, 1928 entry.]

February 1930

February 1 Saturday
Played in snow to-day & made snow cream. Took pictures. Mamma is feeling well. Went to see Wade.

February 2
Went to church this morning & took pictures with Mabel & Wade. Read letter that Leona Spencer wrote to paper about herself. [The editor could not locate this letter in *The Courier* or the *Greensboro Daily News*.]

February 3
Came back [to Elon College] on bus this morning. Talked to Mrs. Charles before I left. Found letter & card from Fred when I got here.

February 4
Stayed with Sapp. Ann Rawls' cousin came to-night—Jane Trottman. Made book report.

February 5
Went to class ball games. Stayed with Sapp. Drew my picture to start painting. Dutch scene.

February 6
Painted all afternoon—Fred came up to studio. Quit smoking.

February 7
Fred & I socialized in studio this afternoon.

February 8 Saturday
Moved up with Sapp. Jimmie [Stewart] sings to me in the studio. [On Vera Annette Sapp, see entry for October 6, 1929. It is not clear what happened to Mary's previous roommate Ruth Doggett. Perhaps they had a dispute and separated, or Ruth did not return to Elon for the spring semester.]

February 9
Went to church this morning & talked to Fred all afternoon. We rode in elevator, or rather hid in it. John came. [Possibly John Crowell.]

February 10
Fred is so good to me.

February 11
Fred & I went down town during Chapel—& socialized to-night—

February 12
Indian Program to-night. Fred & I socialized at corner of store all the time
& everybody down town got caught. [It was a violation of college rules for a
female student to be downtown without a chaperone at times other than the
regularly posted afternoon hours, unless granted special permission from the
dean of women. While downtown, female students, unless accompanied by a
chaperone, were not to talk to males or otherwise socialize with them.[226]]

February 13
Talked to Fred again to-night. He's the sweetest thing in the world. Did he
steal a little kiss? (No, several)

February 14
Got Valentines from John, Ralph & Maxie. [Possibly John Crowell.]

February 15 Saturday
Jimmie told me that every time he sang "Rio Reta" he was singing to me.

February 16
Went to church to-day. Wrote letter to George & cursed him out. Talked
to Fred this afternoon & went to ride to-night. [Probably George Ward of
Asheboro.]

February 17
My hyacinths are beginning to bloom. Wrote Mabel—

Image 67: Mary Auman (*left*) and friends, late 1920s.

February 18
Up before board to-night for being at Burlington last Sat. Campused 14 days. Sapp probated. Talked to Fred. Went to Greensboro & got evening dress.

February 19
Went down town with Fred after girls ball game—

February 20
Junior girls played sophomores. Fred has lab. George Kelly told me that Fred really liked me. [George Kelly, a junior from Durham, North Carolina, was a player on the Elon football team and captain of its basketball team for the 1929–30 season. See also entry for April 11, 1929.[227]]

February 21
Played Lenoir-Rhyne. They beat 33–31. Everybody going home for holiday. Daddy called & said for me to come home.

February 22 Saturday
Went home early this morning. Rode with Mr. & Mrs. Coulter to Greensboro & Howard & Mabel met me there.

February 23
Went to Sunday school. Played horseshoes with Wade [Harris] & Cecil [Leach]. Came back [to Elon College] this aft.

February 24
Fred sent me his I.T.K. bid to-day. [Iota Tau Kappa fraternity.]

February 25
Fred advised me to leave Sapp. We fixed it up. I was to have an attack of appendicitis & have to move down on 2nd.

February 26
Had plenty of fun carrying out our plan—talked to George Kelly some. [It is not clear with whom Mary roomed for the remainder of the semester.]

February 27
Had Freshman-Sophmore banquet to-night in gym. Had lots of fun. I was with Lois McFarland. Fred went to J-S with Wantel. [Wantell Lambeth. "J-S" is probably a reference to a Junior-Senior banquet. On Lois McFarland, see entry for October 29, 1928.]

February 28
Mamma operated on to-day. Fred called me out of the library & we went down town.

February 29
Got letter from Daddy this morning saying Mamma stood operation all right yesterday. Removed large tumor. [Since there was not a "February 29" in 1930, this entry applies to March 1.]

March 1930

March 1 Saturday
B.O.B. Banquet to-night. Everybody stayed out. We danced by their music. Fred & I stayed on the cellar steps most of the time. I played baseball with Fred & George. [Could this be George Ward of Asheboro?]

March 2
Howard, Kivett & Glen came by for me this morning & we went to see Mamma. Had dinner at a cafeteria. Mamma is feeling fine. [Kivett Stuart and Glenn Auman were Mary's cousins from Moore County. A member of the football team, Glenn Auman graduated from Elon College in 1936. He became a math teacher and coach at Hillsboro High School in Orange County. Both were grandsons of Jason Auman (1850–1923) and great-grandsons of Franklin Auman (1826–1911).]

March 3
Went to Burlington & saw "Gold Diggers of Broadway." Sat with Fred. Came back on bus to-night. [*Gold Diggers of Broadway* is a 1929 Warner Brothers musical comedy starring Nancy Welford and Conway Tearle.[228]]

March 4
Up before board for socializing Sat. night with Fred. Went with him to social hour but we stayed outside most of the time.

March 5
Wrote Mamma. Went down town with Fred during chapel.

March 6
Sent Mamma a "Maroone & Gold." Went to Burlington with Jane & saw "City Girl." A car hit me. Went down town with Fred. [The *Maroon and Gold* was the Elon College student weekly newspaper published and edited

primarily by members of the Junior Class. *City Girl* is a 1930 Fox Film Corporation drama starring David Torrence and Edith Yorke.[229]]

March 7
Dean [Savage] caught Jane & I down town. Talked to Fred.

March 8 Saturday
Went to ITK banquet with Fred. Had a wonderful time. Had orchestra & radio program. Fred had "I'm a Dreamer" played to me. He's the sweetest one. Gave little clocks as favors.

Corner of Main and Front streets in 1934

Image 68: Burlington, North Carolina.

March 9
Went to church. Wrote Fred a note & asked if he got my clock. Had date with him this aft. & at church to-night. Went up in balcony & got scared they would catch us.

March 10
Socialized with Fred.

March 11
Up before board & "~~probated~~."

March 12
Fred won't even come around. Seems to be mad. Maybe its because I'm probated.

March 13
I painted a panther in watercolors.

March 14
[No entry.]

March 15 Saturday
Called up Howard but he went home last night. Then I called Daddy & he said for me to come home on bus.

Image 69: Frank Auman house, Seagrove, North Carolina, in 2007 (built in 1913).

March 16
Went to church this morning. Howard, Bood, Wade & Mabel brought me to Greensboro & I came the rest of way [to Elon College] on bus.

March 17
Daddy said to-day that Howard would have to be operated on to-night for appendicitis.

March 18
Howard got along all right. Daddy wrote.

March 19
Didn't see Fred hardly at all.

March 20
Mamma came home to-day. Howard got her room [at the hospital in High Point].

March 21
Can't wait to get home. Went to High Point to see Howard & home with Kizzie & Jimmy.

March 22 Saturday
Mamma is getting along fine. Went to Senior Play at schoolhouse to-night. Nina Bean was so good. Ralph B. came to see me. [On Nina Bean, now age about eighteen, see entry for February 5, 1928.]

March 23
Came back with Lizzie & Jimmie to High Point & saw Howard [at the hospital].

March 24
Fred acts kindly cold. Got letter from John & Clarence. [Clarence Overman of Asheboro; probably John Crowell.]

March 25
Off probation to-night. Played first baseball game with Springfield O. to-day. Went with Lila. [Possibly Springfield, Ohio.]

March 26
Fred called me out of library & he told me A.V. had invited him to her banquet. Darn her!! ["A.V." may have been Anna Virginia Britt. See entries for November 29, 1928, and January 4, 1930.]

March 27
Glee Clubs gave operetta to-night. Fred didn't come for me & I was mad. He came after while & I talked to him. Went to Greensboro & got a red fox fur. Saw "Only the Brave" "Gary C" ["Gary C" refers to Gary Cooper, the star of the 1930 historical Civil War drama released by Paramount Famous Lasky Corporation.[230]]

March 28
Fred came up during social hour & again after while. He is so sweet. Played Davidson [College] & lost. 6–4.

March 29 Saturday
Delta U. Banquet. Fred went with A.V. Dean [Savage] gave a popcorn & bridge party but wouldn't let us go over & hear music. I was worried about Fred. Played tennis & hiked with Polly. [Delta Upsilon Kappa, a sorority.[231]]

Image 70: National Theater on Elm Street at night, Greensboro, North Carolina, about 1946.

March 30
Fred called me down but didn't want to have date because of A.V. She came down town.

March 31
I was worried about Fred & A.V. We went down to the gate & she came by.

April 1930

April 1
Went to the gate with Fred to-night. A.V. came along & Fred "April fooled" me just as she passed. Miss Hunter caught us. [The 1930 Federal Census listed Mary T. Hunter, age about 56, as a "Matron at College." She roomed at a boarding house that contained twelve persons who were employees of Elon College, including six "college professors." The college's dean of women, Louise Savage, age thirty-three, was one of those professors.[232]]

April 2
Fred left with baseball team for Virginia. He drove one car.

Image 71: Fred Caddell, Elon College Basketball Team, 1929–30.

April 3
Got letter from Fred & wrote him. Lost his to-night & Ruth & I had a hot time discussing "who" got it. [Possibly Ruth Doggett. Mary did not follow "lost his" with a noun.]

April 4
Went home this afternoon. Saw "The Vagabond King" in Greens[boro]. Wrote Fred from bus station. [*The Vagabond King* is a 1930 musical released by Paramount Famous Lasky Corporation starring Jeanette MacDonald and Dennis King.[233]]

April 5 Saturday
Mabel & I worked all morning in flower garden. Rode around this aft.

April 6
Rained all morning. Howard brought me back [to Elon College] & went on to Chapel Hill. Didn't see Fred to-night.

April 7
Didn't see Fred all day. Played tennis with Agnes G. Went with Lois & Mode to sorority room & played bridge & danced. [Probably Lois McFarlan and Maedell Lambeth.]

April 8
Played tennis all morning & hiked to an old haunted house in the country & waded in the branch.

April 9
Sapp & L.C. suspended. Painted on my picture. [Mary roomed for about two weeks in February 1930 with Vera Annette Sapp, a junior from Douglas, Georgia. See entries for October 6, 1929, and February 8, 25, and 26, 1930.]

April 10
Fourteen boys & girls suspended. Fred & Archie took two girls to ride. Now they can't play ball for 2 weeks. [That the automobile was seen as a threat to chastity is demonstrated by the following edict from the Elon College student handbook: "Under no circumstances can young men and young women of the College while under College jurisdiction ride with each other in automobiles or other vehicles except on picnics and special occasions." J. Archie Fogleman, a freshman from Snow Camp, North Carolina, was on the Elon College football team.[234]]

April 11
Played tennis a lot to-day. Asked Dean [Savage] to let Fred play with me but she wouldn't.

April 12 Saturday
Played tennis all aft. Went to show—Untamed—to-night. [This is the second time Mary recorded going to see *Untamed*. See entry for January 6, 1930.]

April 13
Went to church. Had date with Fred this afternoon and slipped out to-night. We had to hide & wait till Miss Hunter went down town before we could get in. [On Miss Hunter, see entry for April 1, 1930.]

Image 72: Charles Vernon "Lefty" Briggs, star athlete at Elon College, 1929.

April 14
Went down town to-night with Fred. Dean [Savage] was at a tea and we had a hard time getting in.

April 15
Painted all day on my picture. Ella Garrret gave her recital to-night & Moyde, Ann & I slipped down town & met the boys. [On Moyd Fite, see entry for October 23, 1928. Ella Keyser Garrett was a senior from Elon College, North Carolina.[235]]

April 16
Finished my picture. Met Fred in the Hall & we went down town. Went again with Lucy & Lois. [Probably Lois McFarland.]

April 17
I am eighteen to-day. Mamma sent me box of candy.

April 18
Went home to-day. Went by Greensboro and got a new Chiffon dress.

April 19 Saturday
Ralph Burroughs came to-night & we went to show at Asheboro. George was selling tickets. [Mary is probably referring to George Ward here. Perhaps Mary was dating the Ralph Burroughs who lived in Star, North Carolina, who she lists under "Christmas Cards Sent" at the end of her diary. Perhaps he was also the same Ralph Burroughs, age about nineteen, who was rooming at the residence of Enos Sikes in Asheboro in 1930. Ralph was a laborer at a hosiery mill, and Enos was the owner of a lumberyard.[236]]

April 20
Easter: Went to Grandpa's for dinner. Drove daddy over in the [Uwharrie] Mts. John came to-night. [Probably John Crowell.]

April 21
Gilmer [Auman] brought us back [to Elon College]. Fred & Lefty had it planned to bring me & Alta back but I didn't go to the game at Greensboro Stadium.

April 22–25
[No entry.]

April 26 Saturday
Went to Greensboro & decided to go home with Ruth. George Fields & "Shep" took us. [This is probably a reference to Ruth Doggett, Mary's former roommate at Elon College, who lived in the Summerfield community a few miles north of Greensboro. See entry for October 8, 1929, for information on the Doggetts.]

April 27

Ruth's people went off & we went to Mrs Richard's. Claud Williams & Buck Stafford came over. We danced & Claud & I played. Rode around with Buster & Claud to-night & had lots of fun.

April 28

Claud came early this morning & we rode around till one o'clock & then saw "Montana Moon." Came back to school. [*Mountain Moon* is a 1930 MGM western starring Johnny Mack Brown and Joan Crawford.[237]]

April 29

Fred gone all day and to-morrow. Played tennis. Wore new pink dress with puff sleeves.

April 30

Fred came back to-night. Read "The Little Minister." [A novel written in 1891 by James M. Barrie, author of the play *Peter Pan, the Boy Who Wouldn't Grow Up* (1904).[238]]

May 1930

May 1

Saw Fred this morning & he asked if I was mad at him. Glee Club went to Raleigh & we socialized down town to-night. Slipped in behind Dorm.

May 2

Alta & Lefty planned for Lefty & Fred to come to see us [in Seagrove] Sunday.

May 3 Saturday

Went to Greensboro & met Daddy & Mabel. She got a new blue dress. Vada [Graves] married Lonnie Royall to-day. [Lonnie David Royall (1905–78) lived in High Point, North Carolina, with his parents, Louis and Lula. Louis Royall was a varnisher at a furniture factory, and Lula was an inspector at a hosiery mill. Lonnie was unemployed at the time of the census.[239]]

May 4

Fred & Lefty came down home [i.e., to Seagrove] to see Alta & I. They brought us back after 10 & we went back to Greensboro & stayed with Elizabeth Neil. Fred is the sweetest thing in the world—(excepting nothing). [Fred and Lefty were breaking the following "Red Book" rule here: "Young men of the College are not allowed to call on or be with young lady members of the College off the campus, nor on the campus except as the dean shall suspend regulations."[240]]

May 5
Alta & I came back on the 7:00 o'clock bus. We were afraid Dean [Savage] would find out about us. Fred & I went down town & to Glee Club program with Miss Hunter. [On Miss Hunter, see entry for April 1, 1930.]

May 6
Fred left this morning at 8:00 o'clock Moyde & I went over & saw them leave. [Moyd Fite.]

May 7–18
[No entry.]

May 19
Exams begin. I don't have one to-day.

May 20
Psy. & Education exams. Got along pretty good.

May 21
French exam this morning.

May 22
Slipped off & went to Burlington. Bowled with Moyd, Sally & Kitty all afternoon.

May 23
Johnnie Sharp & I went to Burlington this morning & bowled. Dean Savage looked for me so I had to come back. Fred went on Senior Picnic.

May 24 Saturday
Dean Savage said I had to go home this morning. Alta and I went to Greensboro & Fred & Lefty met us at the King Cotton [Hotel] to-night & brought me home [i.e., to Seagrove]. [Apparently Dean Savage, exasperated by Mary's numerous barefaced violations of the college gender code of conduct as laid out in the "Red Book," kicked Mary out of school.]

May 25
Sunday.

May 26
John Ward came down.

May 27
[No entry.]

Image 73: King Cotton Hotel, 1927, Greensboro, North Carolina.

May 28
Fred went to High Point to play ball.

May 29
[No entry.]

May 30
Fred is playing ball & doing fine.

May 31 Saturday
Got letter from Ruth. [This is probably a reference to Ruth Doggett.]

June 1930

June 1
SAW [spelling unclear], in paper

June 2
Ate first peaches to-day. Bob & I walked down to the dam in our pasture.

Image 74: Mary *(left)* and Mabel Auman, with their Uncle Dave Cornelison
and his 1920 Hudson Six.

June 3
Got two letters from Fred this morning. Got my grades from Elon. Averaged
82-1/2. [Or possibly 89-1/2.]

Image 75: Seagrove in 1935. The first three buildings from left are the Seagrove Café,
Frank Auman Store, and Jasper Auman Store.

June 4
[No entry.]

June 5
John & George Ward, Tom Carey & Edith came to-night.

June 6–9
[No entry.]

June 10
Started staying in the store. [Mary is referring to her father's general store in Seagrove.]

June 11
Howard went to Carolina to summer school.

June 12
Stayed in store.

June 13–16
[No entries.]

June 17
Jim Cagle, John & Romie Harmon, Frank Yow and all the boys have formed a "Loafers Association" in the store.

June 18
Had date with Rufus Reynolds & we went to the show at Asheboro. [Rufus Reynolds, age about twenty-two, was a son of R. Bryant Reynolds, owner of a country store in Moore County. Rufus was a student at Duke University, where he would earn a bachelor of arts and a law degree. After serving in the Judge Advocate General Corps in World War II, he settled in Greensboro, North Carolina, where he served on the bankruptcy bench for the Middle District of North Carolina for forty-two years. On May 27, 1929, Bernice Auman (1903–67), Mary's second cousin, married Swannie Reynolds (1905–2005), a sister of Rufus Reynolds. (On Bernice Auman, see entry for November 18, 1928.) In 1987, A.R. Auman Jr. (1918–2006), Mary's second cousin and a widower, married Rufus Reynolds's sister Geneva (1921–2007), a widow. A.R. Auman Jr. was a graduate of the University of North Carolina and its Navy ROTC program, and captain of a U.S. Navy minesweeper during World War II. He and his brother Hubert Auman, a graduate of North Carolina State College, owned and operated Seagrove Hardware for about fifty years after the death of their father, A.R. Auman Sr., in 1942. They were younger

brothers of Alberta and Mildred Auman. On the family of A.R. Auman Sr., see entry for January 22, 1928.[241]]

June 19–21
[No entries.]

June 22
Went to Aunt Ruth's and down to the pond.

June 23–24
[No entries.]

June 25
Ivey and Ruby married to-day and left for Washington. [Ivey Luck and Ruby Owen. On Ruby Owen, see entry for October 7, 1928.]

June 26
[No entry.]

June 27
Daddy got mad when he saw Jim Slack & me running in the store.

June 28 Saturday
[No entry.]

June 29
Fred came this aft. with Sparky Moore. Mamma & Daddy went to Winston. We had a good time. He stayed till 11:00. [This is likely a reference to Fred Caddell.]

June 30
I can't do anything to-day. Mabel says I'm love-sick. All the boys tease me about being so pale & sleepy. Wrote Fred.

July 1930

July 1
[No entry.]

July 2
Got the sweetest letter from Fred. Wade, Mabel & I ate peaches.

[This is the last daily entry in the diary. What follows in the next chapter is miscellaneous information found in the back of the diary.]

Image 76: Mary Auman, Asheboro, NC, about 1938.

Chapter 5

End Matter

Important Events

"BigSnow   —1927—
Deepest for 70 yrs.—26 in. on level   Night of March 1
Electric Lights in Seagrove   Feb. 1928
Lindbergh Crossed Atlantic   May 21, 1927
"Vitaphone" "Talking Pictures"   Aug. 13, 1928
Entered College   Sept. 3, 1928
Hoover Elected President   Nov. 6, 1928
General Foch died   March 1929
Lindbergh Married Ann Morrow   May 1929

Christmas Cards Sent

Adna Lane Bruton   Mt. Gilead N.C.
Mary Rawls Jones   Holland Va.
Mattie Hudson   Dunn N.C.
J.S. Ferree   Mt. Gilead N.C.
Fred Hill   Mt. Gilead N.C.
Anna Virginia Britt   Holland Va.
Louie Ziegler   Birmingham Ala.
Carl Peters   Appalachia Va.
Elizabeth Slack   Hemp N.C.
Virginia Brown   Hemp N.C.
Julia Mae Bass   Dunn N.C.
Ralph Burroughs   Star N.C.
Nannie Stout   Sanford N.C.
Catherine Lemmond   Sanford N.C.
Curvie Keith   Northside N.C.
Helen Turner   Rocky Mount N.C.

Edith Brower   Asheboro N.C.
Lillie & C. O'Quinn   Star N.C.
Vernitia Stutts   Seagrove N.C.

Christmas Cards Received

Nannie Stout   Sanford
Louie Ziegler   Birmingham Ala.
Adna Lane Bruton   Mt. Gilead
Fred Hill   Mt. Gilead
Ralph Burroughs   Star
Elmer Calicutt   Greensboro
Edwin Hughes   Asheboro
Vernitia Stutts   Seagrove
Edith Brower   Asheboro
Edith McDowell   Asheboro
Lillie & Charlie O'Quinn   Star
Gertrude Paschell   Norlina
Lewis Cagle   Ether
A.A. Rodriquez   Cuba

Birthdays and Anniversaries

July 16, 1911   Vada Graves
Sept. 28, 1910   Martha Graves
Oct. 26, 1910   Alberta Auman
March 16, 1910   Alta Mae Matthews
Oct. 3, 1908   Maple Lawrence
June 19, 1908   Vernitia Stutts
April 17, 1912   Mary Auman
Jan. 14, 1911   Howard Auman
Aug. 23, 1908   Lane Russell
Dec. 21, 1907   Fred Auman
Sept. 27, 1909   Harwood Graves
March 12, 1908   William Matthews
Aug. 30, 1905   Walter Macon
Oct. 3, 1905   Elijah Lucas

Memoranda

May 9, 1928
   Your last day as a "Senior" in high school. Next year a "Freshman." May the same success be yours throughout your college career as you have enjoyed in high school.
   Lena Russell

   "A good name is rather to be chosen than great riches and loving favor rather than silver and gold."
   May life ever be good to you, Mary, and may you live long and ever be the happy sweet girl that you now are.
   L. O'Quinn

   Will you ever forget the nite at Elon College when we were all excited about being sent home on account of the flu!
   I will all ways cherish in my mind, when I am old and gray, the happy days at old Elon. I hope you will sometime, in the future, think of just
   Louise Hough
   West Point, N. Y.
   or
   31 Church Street
   Highland Falls, N.Y.

Frank(lin) Auman—born—July 24, 1883
Mattie Luck Auman   July 24, 1888
   Married   Oct. 3, 1909
Howard Frank(lin) Auman—born—Jan. 14, 1911
Mary Elizabeth Auman—born—April 17, 1912
Clara Mabel Auman—born—Jan. 5, 1914

Moved to Seagrove [from Auman's Crossroads]—March 12, 1913.

Started building new house [in Seagrove] in April [1913] and soon moved into it.

End of Diary

Chapter 6:

Epilogue

On May 24, 1930, the day after final examinations ended in the spring semester, Louise Savage, the dean of women, told Mary that she "had to go home this morning." Two days before, Mary had "slipped off to Burlington," where she went bowling with friends. She did the same the next day but returned to campus when she heard that "Dean Savage looked for me so I had to come back." Dean Savage, furious at Mary's blatant violations of gender protocols as detailed in the *Elon College Handbook*, ordered her to leave campus immediately, never to return. In the fall of 1930, Mary matriculated at the North Carolina College for Women (today, the University of North Carolina at Greensboro).

Mary earned her bachelor's degree in education from Woman's College in 1933, and Howard received his degree in commerce from the University of North Carolina in 1932. Mabel graduated from Woman's College in 1935. (In 1932, the name North Carolina College for Women was changed to The Woman's College of the University of North Carolina.) All three returned to Seagrove to live with their parents. Howard worked with his father in the lumber business. Mary and Mabel taught at the Seagrove School at various times over the years after they graduated from college.

In 1935, Frank Auman built a house in Asheboro on a lot adjacent to the Randolph County Courthouse at the intersection of Worth and Cox Streets. Mary lived with her family in Asheboro until 1938, when she married Howard Sprague (1911–84), a native Texan who was the general superintendent of Randolph Lingerie, a textile mill in Randleman, a small town about six miles north of Asheboro. Howard graduated from Southern Methodist University in 1933 with a degree in commerce; he and two of his brothers were noted members of the SMU football team. Howard's father, George A. Sprague (1871–1963), an entrepreneur engaged in the freight and warehouse business, was the mayor (1937–39) of Dallas, Texas.

Image 77: Frank and Mattie Auman house, Asheboro, North Carolina, about 1937.

Howard and Mary Sprague moved into a bungalow that they built in Asheboro. On June 3, 1940, they had their only child, a son they named Franklin "Frank" Howard Sprague. Mary's life came to a tragic end on March 6, 1949, when she died of liver disease caused by alcohol abuse. Howard Sprague returned to Texas with his son. He married Iona Seals (1904–84) and lived the remainder of his years on his stock farm near Weatherford. His son, Frank, graduated from Texas A&M University in 1963 with a degree in agriculture. That same year, Frank married Katherine Jozwiak; they had two children, Howard David Sprague (1964) and Kathleen Sprague (1966). Upon completing a career working for the United States Department of Agriculture, Frank Sprague retired in 1995 to Hamilton, Texas.

Howard Auman married Lucille Crisp of Candler, North Carolina, in 1938. He bought the Capel place, a two-thousand-acre tract of land in the Auman's Crossroads community where he was born. Noah Smitherman, a planter and owner of thirty-five slaves, owned the tract in antebellum times. Howard built a log cabin on the property and became a cattleman dealing in Holsteins and Herefords; he also engaged in real estate and home construction enterprises. Howard and Lucille Auman had three children: Frank (1940), Bill (1942), and Anne (1944).

After college, Mabel Auman lived with her parents until she married Leonard Teel (1906–81), an electrical contractor in Asheboro. They settled on an eight-hundred-acre tract of land located on the banks of the Little River several miles south of Asheboro near the Charlie Luck farm. There they farmed and raised cattle. They had one child, Frank Auman Teel (1942).

Image 78: Mary Sprague and her son Frankie, 1942.

Image 79: Howard Sprague, mid-1930s.

Image 80: Howard Auman's log cabin built in 1938 on Tantrough Farm, located in the Auman's Crossroads community.

Image 81: *From left,* Mabel, Auman and Leonard Teel, 1954, in Frank Auman house in Asheboro, North Carolina. The oil painting is by Mary Auman.

When Lebbeus Auman retired from the army, he built a house on a lot on the south side of Asheboro. During World War II, his two sons served in the military. His son Thomas Auman, Fireman, First Class, United States Navy, was lost at sea in the Pacific Theater on June 13, 1945, at Okinawa. Samuel married and settled in Asheboro. Evelyn Auman graduated from Woman's College in 1947; she later married and moved to Anniston, Alabama, where she raised two girls. Bertha outlived Lebbeus by about twenty years.

A few years after he married Ruby Owen, Ivey Luck built a brick house across the highway from his business. Ivey and Ruby had one child, Martha, born in 1933. In 1947, Ivey Luck and Alfred Spencer established a small business—The Mountain View Canning Company—that canned meats and vegetables for people in the Seagrove area. In 1950, they began canning beef and gravy for sale to the public, as well as pinto beans. Soon they introduced other meat and vegetable products for sale. In 1953, Alfred Spencer sold his share of the business to Ivey Luck, who changed the name to Luck's Incorporated. The business thereafter grew rapidly. In 1967, Luck's Incorporated merged with American Home Products. Ivey Luck died in 1989 at the age of ninety-one. Descendants buried Ivey and Ruby at the Christian Church cemetery in Seagrove.[242]

Dave Cornelison retired from his retail business around 1950. He and Belle built a house in Asheboro, where they spent the remainder of their lives. After dropping out of college and marrying, Fred Auman moved to Society Hill, South Carolina, where he established a furniture manufacturing company. Alberta Auman graduated from Elon College in 1932. In 1948, she married her Seagrove High School classmate, Lane Russell. Alberta taught in the Seagrove and Asheboro public schools for about forty-five years; Lane owned and operated a hardware store in Asheboro. Mildred Auman married James Bone of Pennsylvania in 1944. James served in combat in the North African, Sicilian, and Italian campaigns during World War II as a soldier in the United States Army. After he suffered a severe wound at Anzio, the Army sent him back to the States to recover. James and Mildred Bone made their home in Seagrove.[243] Upon marrying, Lena Russell became Lena Flennikan. She spent most of her adult life teaching English at Asheboro High School. (In the late 1950s, Bill and Frank Auman, sons of Howard and Lucille Auman, and Auman Teel, son of Mabel and Leonard Teel, were her students at Asheboro High.) After Frank Auman died of a heart attack in 1941, his wife, Mattie, lived alone in their Asheboro home until her death in 1963.

Her family buried Mary Elizabeth Sprague at the Oaklawn Cemetery in Asheboro alongside her father, Frank. Since then, her mother, Mattie Auman; her brother Howard Frank Auman and his wife, Lucille; and her sister Clara Mabel Teel and her husband, Leonard, have joined her there. Also buried at Oaklawn Cemetery, not far from the Frank and Mattie Auman family, are Lebbeus and Bertha Auman, their son Samuel Auman, and Dave and Belle Cornelison.

Image 82: Ivey Luck about 1970; founder of Luck's Incorporated.

Image 83: Mary's son Frank Sprague, 1994.

Image 84: Thomas Auman, U.S. Navy, lost at sea, Pacific Theater, June 13, 1945.

Image 85: Howard and Lucille Auman with their children—*from left*, Bill, Frank, and Anne—Asheboro, North Carolina, 1946.

Photograph Credits

The following images are from the Auman Family Papers #4401, Southern Historical Collection, Wilson Library, University of North Carolina at Chapel Hill: Image numbers 1, 2, 3, 4, 5, 6, 8, 13, 14, 25, 29, 30, 32, 35, 41, 52, 56, 64, 65, 66, 67, 84, 85.

The following images are the property of the Auman family: Image numbers 7, 9 10, 11, 12, 16, 17, 18, 19, 20, 21, 24, 43, 47, 49, 51, 53, 55, 58, 62, 74, 76, 77, 80.

The following images are courtesy of the Elon University Archives and Special Collections Department of Belk Library, *Phi Psi Cli 1928*, *Phi Psi Cli 1929*, and *Phi Psi Cli 1930* yearbook collections: Image numbers 33, 34, 36, 37, 38, 42, 48, 60, 61, 71, 72.

The following images are from the Randolph County Historical Photographs, Randolph County Public Library, Randolph Room, Asheboro, North Carolina, www.randolphlibrary.org/historicphotos.htm: Image numbers 22, 23, 44, 54, 82.

The editor copied the following image from Dorothy and Walter Auman, *Seagrove Area* (Asheboro, North Carolina: Village Printing Company, 1976), p. 169: Image number 26.

The May Memorial Library, Burlington, North Carolina, provided the following images: Image numbers 50, 68.

The Greensboro Historical Museum, Archives Division, Greensboro, North Carolina, provided the following images: Image numbers 39, 40, 70, 73.

Nancy Auman Cunningham provided the following images: Image numbers 27, 28.

Paul Lucas provided the following image: Image number 75.

Frank Sprague provided the following images: Image numbers 78, 79, 83.

Auman Teel provided the following image: Image number 81.

Beulah Luck provided the following image: Image number 63.

Clem Paffe took the following images for the editor: Image number 15, 31, 45, 46, 57, 59, 69.

Notes

1. For a history of the Auman family of North Carolina from 1730 to the present, see William Thomas Auman, "Some Genealogical Problems Relating to the Andrew and Michael Auman Families Which Emigrated from Frederick County, Maryland, to Randolph County, North Carolina, in the 1790s" and "Notes on the Auman Family in Pennsylvania and Maryland" in Mae Caudill Auman, et al., *The Genealogy of the Andrew Auman Family,* 6th ed. (Seagrove, North Carolina: Andrew Auman Family Reunion, 1985), 17–40 and 41–49. See also William Thomas Auman, "Andrew Auman Family History Primer" in Mae Caudill Auman and William Thomas Auman, *The Genealogy of the Andrew Auman Family*, 7th ed. (Seagrove, North Carolina: Andrew Auman Family Reunion, 2008), iii–x.

2. At that time, Guilford College offered high school level courses in its curriculum.

3. The genealogical information on the Auman and allied families in this diary comes from the extensive genealogical research done by Mae Caudell Auman over the past several decades. See Mae Caudill Auman and William Thomas Auman, *The Genealogy of the Andrew Auman Family*, 7th ed. (Seagrove, North Carolina: Andrew Auman Family Reunion, 2008), 1–710.

4. Dorothy and Walter Auman, *Seagrove Area* (Asheboro, North Carolina: Village Printing Company, 1976), 107–112, 115–118, 138. This book has been an invaluable aid in the editing of this diary. It shall hereinafter be cited as Auman, *Seagrove Area*. Walter and Dorothy (née Cole) Auman owned and operated the Seagrove Pottery from 1953 until their sudden deaths in an auto accident in 1991. Dorothy was a daughter of Charles C. Cole, founder of the C.C. Cole Pottery, which operated from 1939 to 1971. Walter was a grandson of Fletcher Auman, owner of a pottery in the early 1900s. In the 1960s, when the area pottery industry was in decline, Dorothy Auman led a successful ad campaign to alert the country at large to the Seagrove Area traditional pottery businesses. Walter and Dorothy Auman's collection of rare Seagrove Area Pottery is on permanent display at the Mint Museum in Charlotte, North Carolina. See Robert C. Lock,

The *Traditional Potters of Seagrove, North Carolina and Surrounding Areas from the 1800s to the Present* (Greensboro, North Carolina: The Antique & Collectibles Press, 1994), 116, 117, 149. Hereinafter cited as Lock, *The Traditional Potters of Seagrove*. On the population of Seagrove, see "Seagrove Town" in 1930 U.S. Census, Population Schedule, Richland Twp., Randolph Cty., North Carolina, E.D. 28, Sheets 1A, 1B, 2A, 2B, 3A, www.ancestry.com (September 3, 2009).

5.   See "Memoranda" section at end of diary.

6.   Auman, *Seagrove Area*, 115, 122, 126, 166.

7.   Ibid., 118–121.

8.   1930 U.S. Census, Population Schedule, Richland Twp., Randolph Cty., North Carolina, E.D. 28, Sheet 2B, Lines 60–62, www.ancestry.com (April 14, 2007).

9.   While it is unclear today where Lebbeus attended military school, it is probable that he went to Oak Ridge Military Institute located near Greensboro in Guilford County.

10. Auman, *Seagrove Area*, 18–19.

11. "Seagrove School Opens Spring Term," *The Courier*, (January 5, 1928): 1, and "Seagrove Honor Roll," *The Courier* (January 26, 1928): 4.

12. Auman, *Seagrove Area*, 123, and 1930 U.S. Census, Population Schedule, Richland Twp., Randolph Cty., North Carolina, E.D. 28, Sheet 1B, Lines 94–96, www.ancestry.com (April 18, 2007).

13. 1920 U.S. Census, Population Schedule, Union Twp., Randolph Cty., North Carolina, E.D. 118, Sheet 1B, Lines 68–71, www.ancestry.com (April 11, 2007).

14. On the Graves family, see 1920 U.S. Census, Population Schedule, Richland Twp., Randolph Cty., North Carolina, E.D. 114, Sheet 8A, Lines 44–50, www.ancestry.com (August 1, 2007). On the Auman family, see 1930 U.S. Census, Population Schedule, Union Twp., Randolph Cty., North Carolina, E.D. 34, Sheets 2B and 3A, Lines 99–100 and 1–5, www.ancestry.com (August 29, 2007), and The General Alumni Association, ed., *The University of North Carolina at Chapel Hill Alumni Directory* (The Kingsport Press: Kingsport, Tennessee, 1975), 39.

15. 1930 U.S. Census, Population Schedule, Richland Twp., Randolph Cty., North Carolina, E.D. 8, Sheet 2B, Lines 67–70, www.ancestry.com (April 4, 2007).

16. Alexander G. Skutt and Robert C. Lock, *The Boxing Register: International Boxing Hall of Fame Official Record Book* (Ithaca, New York: McBooks Press, 1997), 138–139, 142–143.

17. 1930 U.S. Census, Population Schedule, Richland Twp., Randolph Cty., E.D. 28, Sheet 1B, Lines 89–91, www.ancestry.com (September 29, 2007), and Auman, *Seagrove Area*, 123.

18. "Seagrove Honor Roll" in *The Courier* (January 26, 1928): 4.

19. For Edith McDowell, see 1920 U.S. Census, Population Schedule, Asheboro Twp., Randolph Cty., North Carolina, E.D. 96, Sheet 10B, Lines 70–73, www.ancestry.com (April 4, 2007). For Edith Brower, see 1930 U.S. Census, Population Schedule, Asheboro Twp., Randolph Cty., North Carolina, E.D. 4, Sheet 3B, Line 92, www.ancestry.com (April 4, 2007). For Alberta Auman, see 1930 U.S. Census, Population Schedule, Richland Twp., Randolph Cty., North Carolina, E.D. 28, Sheet 1A, Lines 1–8, www.ancestry.com (April 11, 2007), and Auman *Seagrove Area*, 121, 126.

20. Boodie Horatio Bean in *North Carolina Death Collection, 1908–1996*, and 1920 U.S. Census, Population Schedule, Union Twp., Randolph Cty., North Carolina, E.D. 118, Sheet 4B, Line 64, www.ancestry.com (September 9, 2007).

21. Auman, *Seagrove Area*, 123, and 1920 U.S. Census, Population Schedule, Richland Twp., Randolph Cty., North Carolina, E.D. 114, Sheet 14B, Lines 90–94, www.ancestry.com (April 5, 2007).

22. "Growth And Influence Of The Christian Endeavor Society," *The Christian Sun*, Elon College, North Carolina (November 23, 1899): 1.

23. "Hostesses To Society—Misses O'Quinn and Lawrence Entertain Christian Endeavor" in *The Courier* (February 9, 1928): 8, and 1920 U.S. Census, Population Schedule, Richland Twp., Randolph Cty., North Carolina, E.D. 114, Sheet 94, Lines 40–44, www.ancestry.com (April 5, 2007).

24. "Hostesses To Society" in *The Courier* (February 9, 1928): 8.

25. 1920 U.S. Census, Population Schedule, Richland Twp., Randolph Cty., North Carolina, E.D. 114, Sheet 10B, Lines 53–54, www.ancestry.com (August 30, 2007).

26. "Seagrove No Longer In Darkness—Now Has 20 Street Lights" in *The Courier* (February 23, 1928): 1.

27. Ibid. On pro-Union and pro-Lincoln sentiment in the Randolph County area during the Civil War, see William T. Auman, "Bryan Tyson: Southern Unionist and American Patriot," *North Carolina Historical Review*, LXII (July, 1985), 257-292. See also, William T. Auman and David D. Scarboro, "The Heroes of America in Civil War North Carolina," *North Carolina Historical Review*, LVIII (October, 1981), 327-363.

28. 1920 U.S. Census, Population Schedule, Biscoe Twp., Montgomery Cty., North Carolina, E.D. 71, Sheet 14B, Lines 65–71, and 1930 U.S. Census, Population Schedule, Richland Twp., Randolph Cty.,

North Carolina, E.D. 8, Sheet 1B, Lines 72–75, www.ancestry.com (September 9, 2007).

29. 1930 U.S. Census, Population Schedule, Richland Twp., Randolph Cty., North Carolina, E.D. 28, Sheet 2B, Lines 71–79, www.ancestry.com (April 5, 2007), and Auman, *Seagrove Area*, 123.

30. 1920 U.S. Census, Population Schedule, Tabernacle Twp., Randolph Cty., North Carolina, E.D. 115, Sheet 8A, Line 47, www.ancestry.com (April 5, 2007).

31. "Richland Township Singing Convention Draws Large Crowd" in *The Courier* (December 3, 1928): 6.

32. 1920 U.S. Census, Population Schedule, Richland Twp., Randolph Cty., North Carolina, E.D. 114, Sheet 10B, Lines 95–100, www.ancestry.com (April 7, 2007).

33. See John L. Andriot, compiler and editor, *Population Abstract of the United States,* Vol. 1, Tables (McLean, Virginia: Andriot Associates, 1983), 574. Hereinafter cited as Andriot, *Population Abstract of the United States.*

34. 1930 U.S. Census, Population Schedule, Asheboro Twp., Randolph Cty., North Carolina, E.D. 3, Sheet 9B, Lines 89–94, www.ancestry.com (April 7, 2007).

35. 1930 U.S. Census, Population Schedule, Richland Twp., Randolph Cty., North Carolina, E.D. 28, Sheet 2B, Lines 57–59, www.ancestry.com (April 9, 2007), and Auman, *Seagrove Area*, 123.

36. "Seagrove News" in *The Courier* (March 22, 1928): 4.

37. On the Yows, see 1920 U.S. Census, Richland Twp., Randolph Cty., North Carolina, E.D. 114, Sheet 9B, Lines 55–60, www.ancestry.com (August 29, 2007).

38. 1920 U.S. Census, Population Schedule, Union Twp., Randolph Cty., North Carolina, E.D. 118, Sheet 4B, Lines 97–100, and Sheet 5A, Lines 1–7, www.ancestry.com (October 10, 2007).

39. 1930 U.S. Census, Population Schedule, Biscoe Twp., Montgomery Cty., North Carolina, E.D. 4, Sheet 10B, Line 61, www.ancestry.com (September 9, 2007).

40. See William S. Powell, *North Carolina Through Four Centuries* (Chapel Hill and London: University of North Carolina Press, 1989), 311–313. Hereinafter cited as Powell, *North Carolina.*

41. About the Plank Road, see Powell, *North Carolina*, 305.

42. *The Phi Psi Chi 1929,* Vol. XV (Senior Class of Elon College: Elon College, North Carolina), 26. Hereinafter cited as *Phi Psi Chi 1929.*

43. 1920 U.S. Census, Population Schedule, Richland Twp., Randolph Cty., North Carolina, E.D. 114, Sheet 10A, Lines 32–34, www.ancestry.com (April 11, 2007).

44. Captain D.C. Green to Colonel McAlister, March 22 and 27, 1865, Alexander Carey McAlister Papers, # 1861, in the Southern Historical Collection at the University of North Carolina at Chapel Hill. For an account of the conflict between the deserter bands and Confederate authorities in the Randolph County Area during the Civil War, see William T. Auman, "Neighbor Against Neighbor: The Inner Civil War in the Randolph County Area of Confederate North Carolina," *North Carolina Historical Review*, LXI (January, 1984), 59-92.

45. On the J.B. Cole Pottery, see Lock, *The Traditional Potters of Seagrove*, 109–126. See also 1930 U.S. Census, Population Schedule, Richland Twp., Randolph Cty., North Carolina, E.D. 7, Sheet 5A, Lines 19–23, www.ancestry.com (April 11, 2007), and Philmore Graves in *North Carolina Marriage Collection, 1741–2004*, www.ancestry.com (July 18, 2007).

46. 1930 U.S. Census, Population Schedule, Appalachia, Wise Cty., Virginia, E.D. 18, Sheet 28A, Lines 1–6, www.ancestry.com (July 17, 2007), and "Seagrove News," *The Courier* (July 19, 1928): 8.

47. "Local—Personal—Society," *The Courier* (September 6, 1928): 5.

48. *U.S. Catalog of Copyright Entries (Renewals) Dramatic Material from 1923 Titles starting with M to R*, www.ibiblio.org./ccer/1923d3.htm (April 17, 2007), and "Seagrove School Graduates Class of Fourteen Members," *The Courier* (May 17, 1928): 2.

49. Andriot, *Population Abstract of the United States*, 574.

50. *Rook*, www.pagat.com/kt5/rook.html (August 20, 2009).

51. From *The Courier*: "Papers Read At Senior Class Day Exercises Asheboro High School" (June 7, 1928): 2–3; "Several Asheboro Boys And Girls To Leave For College" (September 13, 1928): 1; "Democrat Party Presents Strong Ticket To The People of Randolph" (October 25, 1928): 1. See also 1930 U.S. Census, Population Schedule, Asheboro Twp., Randolph Cty., North Carolina, E.D. 4, Sheet 1A, Lines 22–24 (Davis Cranford), and 1920 U. S. Census, Population Schedule, Asheboro Twp., Randolph Cty., North Carolina, E.D. 96, Sheet 17A, Lines 1–4 (Penn Wood Redding), www.ancestry.com (April 12, 2007).

52. "Papers Read At Senior Class Day Exercises," *The Courier* (June 7, 1928): 2–3. See also "Local—Personal—Society," *The Courier* (September 20, 1928): 5, and 1920 U.S. Census, Population Schedule, Asheboro Twp., Randolph Cty., North Carolina, E.D. 96, Sheet 9A, Lines 20–26 (Joe Parrish), and E.D. 96, Sheet 16B, Lines 59–64 (Henry Redding), and 1910 U.S. Census, Population Schedule, Asheboro Twp., Randolph Cty., North Carolina, E.D. 76, Sheet 10B, Lines 73–75 (Thomas Henry Redding), www.ancestry.com (April 13, 2007).

53. "Seagrove News," *The Courier* (June 7, 1928): 8.

54. From *The Courier*: "23 Seniors Are Graduated From Asheboro School" (May 31, 1928): 1; "Papers Read At Senior Class Day Exercises Asheboro High School" (June 7, 1928): 2–3; and "Several Asheboro Boys And Girls To Leave For College" (September 13, 1928): 1.

55. Auman, *Seagrove Area*, 123, and 1930 U.S. Census, Population Schedule, Richland Twp., Randolph Cty., North Carolina, E.D. 8, Sheet 2B, Lines 67–70, www.ancestry.com (April 4, 2007). See also "Seagrove News," *The Courier* (September 6, 1928): 5.

56. For a fascinating account of the history of string bands and the development of fiddlers' conventions in the Piedmont of North Carolina in the twentieth century, see Bob Carlin, *String Bands in the North Carolina Piedmont* (Jefferson, North Carolina: McFarland and Company, 2004).

57. From *The Courier*: "Miss Lyde Bingham And Mr. Euclid Auman Married" (June 21, 1928): 1; "Why Not News" (May 17, 1928): 1; "Prof Harvey White Is Re-Elected Head Of Seagrove School" (June 20, 1929): 1. See also *The Phi Psi Chi 1927*, Vol. XIII (Senior Class of Elon College: Elon College, North Carolina), 36, and 1910 U.S. Census, Population Schedule, Richland Twp., Randolph Cty., North Carolina, E.D. 97, Sheet 11B, Lines 70–76, www.ancestry.com (September 12, 2007).

58. "Seagrove News," *The Courier* (June 14, 1928): 5.

59. Information on *The Big Parade* and all movies discussed in this diary is taken from Turner Classic Movies online "Movie Database" located at www.tcm.com/index.jsp (March 2, 2007), hereinafter cited as TCM Movie Database.

60. 1930 U.S. Census, Population Schedule, Asheboro Twp., Randolph Cty., North Carolina, E.D. 4, Sheet 7A, Lines 47–50, www.ancestry.com (April 13, 2007). See also, from *The Courier*: "Papers Read At Senior Class Day Exercises" (June 7, 1928): 2–3, and "23 Seniors Are Graduated From Asheboro School" (May 31, 1928): 1.

61. Nancy Auman Cunningham of Atlanta, Georgia provided biographical information on Jason and Sarah Auman. Nancy got most of her data from Connie Auman Miller, a daughter of Jason and Sarah Auman. On Jason Auman in 1880, see 1880 U.S. Census, Population Schedule, Union Twp., Randolph Cty., North Carolina, E.D. 224, Page 13, Lines 9–12, www.ancestry.com (10 October 2009). On Jason Auman's death, see *North Carolina Death Certificates, 1909–1975*, www.ancestry.com (14 October 2009). See also "Jason Auman" in Sarah Currie Thompson, *Coming Home to Jackson Springs: A Compilation of Family Stories and Histories, 1750–1950* (Jackson Springs, North Carolina: The Jackson Springs Historical Foundation, Inc., 2006), 40–41.

62. "Hal W. Walker Dies In A Sanford Hospital," *The Courier* (July 12, 1928): 1, and Randle Brim, "The Story of Asheboro's Company 'K,'" *The Heritage of Randolph County North Carolina,* Vol. 2 (Randolph County Heritage Book Committee: Asheboro, North Carolina, 1999), 529–30.

63. "Seagrove News," *The Courier* (July 5, 1928).

64. "Seagrove News," *The Courier* (July 12, 1928): 4

65. Ibid.

66. "First Meeting Of Richland Township Singing Convention Held At Why Not Church Last Sunday With Singers Present From Many Places," *The Courier* (July 19, 1928): 8.

67. 1920 U.S. Census, Population Schedule, Richland Twp., Randolph Cty., North Carolina, E.D. 114, Sheet 15A, Line 11, www.ancestry.com (April 13, 2007), and 1930 U.S. Census, Population Schedule, Richland Twp., Randolph Cty., North Carolina, E.D. 29, Sheet 10A, Lines 14–18, www.ancestry.com (October 10, 2007).

68. 1930 U.S. Census, Population Schedule, Chapel Hill Twp., Orange Cty., North Carolina, E.D. 7, Sheet 3A, Lines 27–32, www.ancestry.com (April 13, 2007).

69. 1920 U.S. Census, Population Schedule, Richland Twp., Randolph Cty., North Carolina, E.D. 114, Sheet 14A, Lines 18–25, www.ancestry.com (April 13, 2007).

70. 1930 U.S. Census, Population Schedule, Richland Twp., Randolph Cty., North Carolina, E.D. 28, Sheet 1A, Lines 15–21, www.ancestry.com (April 13, 2007).

71. 1920 U.S. Census, Population Schedule, Richland Twp., Randolph Cty., North Carolina, E.D. 114, Sheet 10A, Lines 12–14, www.ancestry.com (April 13, 2007).

72. "Dr. Sumner Reports 108 Cases Measles In Randolph County," *The Courier* (April 5, 1928): 1.

73. "Mr. Charles Buys New Gap Station," *The Courier* (February 9, 1928): 5.

74. TCM Movie Database.

75. "Primitive Baptists Hold Associational Meet [At] Suggs Creek," *The Courier* (August 30, 1928): 1; 1930 US Census, Population Schedule, Mineral Springs Twp., Richmond Cty., North Carolina, E.D. 8, Sheet 1B, Lines 70–73, and Connie Auman Miller in *North Carolina Death Collection*, 1908–1996, www.ancestry.com (September 17, 2007).

76. "Seagrove News," *The Courier* (September 6, 1928): 5, and (August 30, 1928): 3.

77. On requiring students to attend church and Sunday school, see Dean A. L. Hook, ed., *Elon College Handbook,* Vol. VII, 1928–29 (Elon College, NC: Elon College, 1928), 47. Hereinafter cited as

Elon College Handbook. On the history of the Christian Church, see Durward T. Stokes and William T. Scott, *A History of the Christian Church in the South* (Burlington, NC: Southern Conference UCC, United Church of Christ, 1975), v, 1–36. Hereinafter cited as Stokes and Scott, *History of the Christian Church.* See also, Durward T. Stokes, *Elon College: Its History and Traditions* (Elon College Alumni Association: Elon College, NC, 1982), 3–4. Hereinafter cited as Stokes, *Elon College.*

78. "Salting beds" was the practice of clandestinely entering a room and adding a quantity of salt between the sheets of the beds. It is unclear what "stacking" a room entailed.

79. *Elon College Handbook*, 25–26, 28–29, 33–37.

80. Ibid., 19–22, 32.

81. *The Phi Psi Chi 1930*, Vol. XVI (Senior Class of Elon College: Elon College, North Carolina), 25. Hereinafter cited as *Phi Psi Chi 1930*

82. *Elon College Handbook*, 7.

83. *Phi Psi Chi 1929*, 71.

84. "Seagrove School Begins Fall Term With 225 Pupils—Prof. Harvey White In Charge," *The Courier* (September 13, 1928): 1.

85. *Phi Psi Chi 1929*, 73

86. Ibid. 67.

87. On Elizabeth Slack, see 1930 U.S. Census, Population Schedule, Scheffields Twp., Moore Cty., North Carolina, E.D. 8, Sheet 9A, Lines 29–34, www.ancestry.com (April 17, 2007). On Alberta Covington, see *Phi Psi Chi 1929*, 72.

88. *Elon College Handbook*, 6.

89. TCM Movie Database and *Phi Psi Chi 1929*, 49. On the population of Burlington, see Andriot, *Population Abstract of the United States,* 574.

90. "Opening Day Of Fair Attended By A Large Crowd," *The Courier* (September 27, 1928): 1, 8.

91. *Phi Psi Chi 1929*, 26 for Colclough and 59 for McPherson.

92. "Dr. J.T. Burrus To Deliver Address At Seagrove, Oct. 2nd," *The Courier* (September 27, 1928): 1.

93. *Phi Psi Chi 1929*, 64.

94. "Sgt. Lebbeus Auman Recovering From Serious Illness," *The Courier* (October 11, 1928): 2.

95. On the Ben Owen pottery, see www.benowenpottery.com, and Lock, *The Traditional Potters of Seagrove*, 152–154.

96. *Maroon and Gold*, Elon College, NC (February 28, 1929): 1, and *Phi Psi Chi 1929*, 124.

97.   TCM Movie Database.
98.   *Phi Psi Chi 1929*, 72.
99.   From *Greensboro Daily News*, Greensboro, NC, (October 12, 1928): "Greensboro Shouts For Smith; Democratic Nominee Says Never Received Better Reception; Expects To Carry State And The Nation; Spends 30 Minutes Here," 1–2, and "Thousands Of Tar Heels Pull And Tug At Al Smith As He Rides Over State," 1–3.
100. *Phi Psi Chi 1929*, 58 (Eure), 57 (Barrett).
101. "Richmond Smothers Elon By 34–0," *Greensboro Daily News* (October 12, 1929, Section 4): 1. On Zeigler, see 1920 U.S. Census, Population Schedule, Birmingham, Jefferson Twp., Alabama, E.D. 19, Sheet 22A, Lines 27–31, www.ancestry.com (July 18, 2007).
102. *Phi Psi Chi 1929*, 64. See also 1920 U.S. Census, Population Schedule, Charlotte, Mecklenburg Cty., North Carolina, E.D. 129, Sheet 3B, Lines 54–61, www.ancestry.com (July 18, 2007).
103. *Phi Psi Chi 1929*, 23.
104. *Elon College Handbook*, 6.
105. Ibid., 37.
106. TCM Movie Database. "The Singing Fool Is Here 3 More Days," *Greensboro Daily News* (October 28, 1928, Section C): 8. On the McFarlands, see *Greensboro, North Carolina, City Directory 1928* (Hill Directory Company: Richmond, Virginia, 1928), 361, and 1920 U.S. Census, Population Schedule, Gilmer Twp., Guilford Cty., North Carolina, E.D. 37, Sheet 3A, Lines 21–26, www.ancestry.com (April 17, 2007). On Roberts and Stout, see *Phi Psi Chi 1929*, 46 (Roberts), 77 (Stout).
107. On Mary Rawles Jones, see *Phi Psi Chi 1929*, 65. On Coach Walker, see Stokes, *Elon College*, 234.
108. *Phi Psi Chi 1929*, 26.
109. Ibid., 82.
110. On Louise Savage, see Stokes, *Elon College*, 225.
111. 1910 US Census, Population Schedule, Union Twp., Randolph Cty., North Carolina, E.D. 100, Sheet 10A, Lines 4–9, www.ancestry.com (September 17, 2007).
112. *Elon College Handbook*, 35, 37.
113. Ibid., 6.
114. "Dominoes," *Encyclopedia Britannica 2007 Ultimate Reference Suite* (Chicago: Encyclopedia Britannica, 2009).
115. "Kelly, George," *Encyclopædia Britannica 2007 Ultimate Reference Suite* (Chicago: Encyclopædia Britannica, 2007).
116. *Phi Psi Chi 1929*, 71.
117. *Phi Psi Chi 1930*, 24.

118. *Phi Psi Chi 1929*, 74.

119. Ibid., 79.

120. TCM Movie Database.

121. *Phi Psi Chi 1929*, 47.

122. 1910 U.S. Census, Population Schedule, Richland Twp., Randolph Cty., North Carolina, E.D. 97, Sheet 5B, Lines 94–100, www.ancestry. com (September 25, 2007).

123. "Seagrove News," *The Courier* (September 6, 1928): 5.

124. 1930 U.S. Census, Population Schedule, Brower Twp., Randolph Cty., North Carolina, E.D. 7, Sheet 8A, Lines 33–34, www.ancestry. com (September 25, 2007).

125. TCM Movie Database. "Announcements," *The Courier* (November 22, 1928): 2.

126. *Phi Psi Chi 1929*, 71, 77.

127. TCM Movie Database.

128. *Phi Psi Chi 1929*, 34.

129. From *Greensboro Daily News*: "Opera Week Opens In Blaze Of Glory Here" (January 15, 1929): 1, 9; "San Carlos Company Presents Two More Excellent Operas" (January 16, 1929): 16; and "North Carolinas' Social Elite Present At Opening Of Opera" (January 16, 1929): 9.

130. TCM Movie Database. On Chandler, see 1930 U.S. Census, Population Schedule, Elon College, Alamance Cty., North Carolina, E.D. 3, Sheet 4A, Line 35, www.ancester.com (October 15, 2007).

131. On Howsare, see *Maroon and Gold* (January 24, 1929): 1. Copies of *Maroon and Gold* are on file in the Elon University Archives and Special Collections Department of Belk Library.

132. *Elon College Handbook*, 7, 26.

133. *Phi Psi Chi 1929*, 78 (Yates), 60 (Underwood and Wicker).

134. TCM Movie Database.

135. *Phi Psi Chi 1929*, 77 (Smith), 60 (Wicker).

136. *Elon College Handbook*, 6.

137. *Phi Psi Chi 1929*, 66, and *Elon College Handbook,* 29, 34.

138. *Elon College Handbook,* 18, 29.

139. *Maroon and Gold* (February 14, 1929): 1.

140. TCM Movie Database.

141. *Maroon and Gold* (February 7, 1929): 1. *Phi Psi Chi 1929*, 87, 95. U.S. Census, Population Schedule, Gilmer Twp., Guilford Cty, North Carolina, E.D. 43, Sheet 19B, Lines 79–86, and Charles Vernon Briggs Jr. in *North Carolina Birth Index 1800–2000* and *North Carolina Death Collection 1908–1996*, www.ancestry.com (July 23, 2007).

142. *Phi Psi Chi 1929*, 75.

143. TCM Movie Database.
144. Ibid.
145. *Phi Psi Chi 1929*, 71.
146. TCM Movie Database.
147. 1920 U.S. Census, Population Schedule, Ward 5, North Danville, Virginia, E.D. 41, Sheet 9B, Lines 76–81, www.ancestry.com (April 21, 2007).
148. *Skinny* in *Internet Movie Database* at www.imdb.com (April 21, 2007).
149. *Phi Psi Chi 1929*, 49.
150. Ibid., 78.
151. *Elon College Handbook*, 6.
152. *Phi Psi Chi 1929*, 40.
153. *Elon College Handbook*, 13.
154. *Phi Psi Chi 1929*, 43 (Locky), 49 (Spoon).
155. Ibid., 78 (Yates), 72 (Coghill).
156. TCM Movie Database, and *Phi Psi Chi 1929*, 67.
157. *Phi Psi Chi 1929*, 64 (Dofflemyer), 77 (Smith).
158. TCM Movie Database. On the Crotts, see 1930 U.S. Census, Population Schedule, Asheboro Twp., Randolph Cty., North Carolina, E.D. 3, Sheet 9B, Lines 76–86, www.ancestry.com (April 21, 2007).
159. Auman, *Seagrove Area*, 115.
160. TCM Movie Database.
161. *The Walter W. Naumburg Foundation, Inc., Previous Winners, Competition Winners, 1925*, www.naumburg.org/previous-winners. php (April 21, 2007).
162. *Phi Psi Cli 1929*, 71.
163. On the Newmans, see 1930 U.S. Census, Population Schedule, Elon College, Alamance Cty., North Carolina, E.D. 3, Sheet 2B, Lines 94–98, www.ancestry.com (July 28, 2007), and *Phi Psi Chi 1929*, 22, 25. On George Kelly and John Lowry, see *Phi Psi Chi 1929*, 59 (Kelly), 66 (Lowry). On Mrs. C. C. Johnson, see *Phi Psi Chi 1929*, 26.
164. TCM Movie Database.
165. *Phi Psi Chi 1929*, 76 (both Richardsons).
166. 1930 U.S. Census, Population Schedule, Union Twp., Randolph Cty., North Carolina, E.D. 34, Sheet 9A, Lines 45–46, www.ancestry.com (April 21, 2007).
167. TCM Movie Database, and *Phi Psi Chi 1929*, 77 (Smith), 83 (Hartly).

168. "Sam Walter Foss: Minor Poet with a Major Message," St. Louis Ethical Society Online Library, www.ethicalstl.org/platforms/platform071199.shtml (October 19, 2007).

169. "Seagrove School Began Fall Term With 225 Pupils," *The Courier* (September 13, 1928): 1, and 1930 U.S. Census, Population Schedule, Coleridge Twp, Randolph Cty, North Carolina, E.D. 9, Sheet 7B, Lines 55–61, www.ancestry.com (September 25, 2007).

170. *PhiPsiCli, 1929*, 34.

171. Ibid., 73.

172. Ibid., 57.

173. Ibid., 59.

174. TCM Movie Database.

175. 1920 U.S. Census, Population Schedule, Boon Station Twp., Alamance Cty., North Carolina, E.D. 4, Sheet 7A, Lines 38–43, www.ancestry.com (April 22, 2007). Elon College was located in Boon Station Township.

176. 1930 U.S. Census, Population Schedule, Richland Twp., Randolph Cty., North Carolina, E.D. 114, Sheet 14A, Lines 11–17, www.ancestry.com (April 21, 2007).

177. "Bridge," *Encyclopedia Britannica 2007 Ultimate Reference Suite* (Chicago: Encyclopedia Britannica, 2009).

178. *Phi Psi Chi 1929*, 73.

179. *Elon College Handbook*, 7.

180. 1930 U.S. Census, Population Schedule, Sand Hill Twp., Moore Cty., North Carolina, E.D. 21, Sheet 13A, Lines 11–14, www.ancestry.com (September 17, 2007).

181. "Asheboro To Stage Biggest July 4th Celebration In History Of Randolph," *The Courier* (June 27, 1929): 1, and "City Celebrated Independence Day With Fine Program," *The Courier* (July 11, 1929): 1. On Talmadge Brown, see 1930 U.S. Census, Population Schedule, Asheboro Twp., Randolph Cty., North Carolina, E.D. 1, Sheet 6A, Lines 8–21, www.ancestry.com (April 21, 2007). On the brothers John and George Ward, see 1930 U.S. Census, Population Schedule, Asheboro Twp., Randolph Cty., North Carolina, E.D. 1, Sheet 4A, Lines 45–50, www.ancestry.com (April 21, 2007).

182. 1930 U.S. Census, Population Schedule, Asheboro, Randolph Cty., North Carolina, E.D. 1, Line 100, Sheet 8B, and Lines 1–4, Sheet 9A, www.ancestry.com (September 26, 2007).

183. "Jethro Almond: 60 Years in Show Business," *Bandwagon*, Vol. 3, No. 2 (Mar–Apr): 18, on *Circus Historical Society* website, www.circushistory.org/index.htm (April 21, 2007).

184. 1920 U.S. Census, Population Schedule, Richland Twp., Randolph Cty., North Carolina, E.D. 114, Sheet 17A, Lines 26–33, www.ancestry.com (April 21, 2007).

185. "Seagrove News," *The Courier* (July 11, 1929): 4.

186. 1920 U.S. Census, Population Schedule, Asheboro Twp., Randolph Cty., North Carolina, E.D. 96, Sheet 13A, Line 1, www.ancestry.com (April 21, 2007), and 1930 U.S. Census, Population Schedule, Manhattan, New York, New York, E.D. 250, Sheet 2B, Line 58, www.ancestry.com (April 22, 2007). "Local—Personal—Society," *The Courier* (January 26, 1928): 5.

187. For Helen and Betsy, see 1930 US Census, Population Schedule, Badin, Albemarle Twp., Stanley Cty., North Carolina, E.D. 16, Sheet 12B, Lines 51–60; for Everett Luck, see 1930 U.S. Census, Population Schedule, San Bernardino, San Bernardino Cty., California, E.D. 93, Sheet 12B, Line 83, www.ancestry.com (August 15, 2007), and Randle Brim, "The Story of Asheboro's Company 'K,'" *The Heritage of Randolph County North Carolina,* Vol. 2 (Randolph County Heritage Book Committee: Asheboro, North Carolina, 1999), 514–35, especially 529.

188. On the Elmer Rich family, see Auman, *Seagrove Area,* 126, and 1920 U.S. Census, Population Schedule, Asheboro Twp., Randolph Cty., North Carolina, E.D. 96, Sheet 11B, Lines 62–68, www.ancestry.com (April 22, 2007).

189. "The Toddle," *Dance History Archives,* www.streetswing.com (April 22, 2007).

190. 1930 U.S. Census, Population Schedule, Hanover, York Cty., Pennsylvania, E.D. 32, Sheet 18A, Line 5, www.ancestry.com (November 3, 2007).

191. *Elon College Handbook,* 27–28.

192. 1930 U.S. Census, Population Schedule, Richland Twp., Randolph Cty., North Carolina, E.D. 28, Sheets 2B & 3A, Lines 96–100 and 1–4, www.ancestry.com (August 28, 2007).

193. 1930 U.S. Census, Population Schedule, Asheboro Twp., Randolph Cty., North Carolina, E.D. 3, Sheet 2A, Line 31, www.ancestry.com (April 22, 2007).

194. TCM Movie Database.

195. Ibid., and *Phi Psi Chi 1930,* 80.

196. TCM Movie Database.

197. Ibid.

198. On Barton College, see www.barton.edu/geninfo/hist_vision.htm (September 9, 2009).

199. *Phi Psi Chi 1930*, 60.
200. Ibid., 80. See Thomas and Lula Doggett in 1900 U.S. Census, Population Schedule, Summerfield, Guilford Cty., North Carolina, E.D. 69, Sheet 6B, Lines 55–56, and Lula and Ruth Doggett in 1930 U.S. Census, Population Schedule, Bruce Twp., Guilford Cty., North Carolina, E.D. 1, Lines 25–26, www.ancestry.com (August 31, 2007).
201. *Phi Psi Chi 1930*, 42.
202. TCM Movie Database.
203. Stokes and Scott, *History of the Christian Church*, 1–19. See also, Elon University Archives Online Resources, "Elon College Founded by the Christian Church," http://org.elon.edu/archives/church.html (April 22, 2007).
204. "Thousands Are In Attendance At The Annual Randolph County Fair Here," *The Courier* (October 17, 1929): 4.
205. 1930 U.S. Census, Population Schedule, Elon College, Alamance Twp., North Carolina, E.D. 3, Sheet 3B, Lines 60–66, www.ancestry.com (July 28, 2007).
206. TCM Movie Database.
207. On the Bank of Seagrove, see Auman, *Seagrove Area*, 126–130.
208. TCM Movie Database.
209. Ibid.
210. *Phi Psi Chi 1930*, 58.
211. "Thurman Cox Dies As Result Of Burns Received Sunday," *The Courier* (November 14, 1929): 1. See also 1920 U.S. Census, Population Schedule, Union Twp., Randolph Cty., North Carolina, E.D. 118, Sheet 5B, Lines 64–70, www.ancestry.com (April 22, 2007).
212. On C. James and Zenith Hurst Velie, see *Elon College Handbook*, 6.
213. *Phi Psi Chi 1930*, 26.
214. Ibid., 44.
215. *Illusions* (1929) in *The Internet Movie Database*, www.imdb.com (April 22, 2007).
216. *Phi Psi Chi 1930*, 26.
217. TCM Movie Database.
218. Ibid.
219. *Phi Psi Chi 1930*, 61.
220. TCM Movie Database.
221. Ibid.
222. Ibid.
223. Ibid., and *Phi Psi Chi 1930*, 71.
224. *Phi Psi Chi 1930*, 71.

225. Ibid., 44.

226. *Elon College Handbook*, 26–27, 35–37.

227. *Phi Psi Chi 1930*, 59, 92, 95.

228. TCM Movie Database.

229. *Elon College Handbook*, 13, and TCM Movie Database.

230. TCM Movie Database.

231. *Phi Psi Chi 1930*, 159.

232. 1930 U.S. Census, Population Schedule, Elon College, Alamance Cty., North Carolina, E.D. 3, Sheet 4A, Line 36, www.ancestry.com (October 18, 2007).

233. TCM Movie Database.

234. *Elon College Handbook*, 35. On Fogleman, see *Phi Psi Chi 1930*, 80, 93.

235. *Phi Psi Chi 1930*, 41.

236. 1930 U.S. Census, Population Schedule, Asheboro Twp., Randolph Cty., North Carolina, E.D. 3, Sheet 3A, Lines 9–14, www.ancestry.com (April 23, 2007).

237. TCM Movie Database.

238. "Barrie, Sir James (Matthew), Baronet," *Encyclopædia Britannica 2007 Ultimate Reference Suite* (Chicago: Encyclopædia Britannica, 2007).

239. See 1930 U.S. Census, Population Schedule, High Point, Guilford Cty., North Carolina, E.D. 57, Sheet 10A, Lines 32–39, and Lonnie David Royall in *North Carolina Death Collection, 1908–1996*, www.ancestry.com (July 30, 2007).

240. *Elon College Handbook*, 35.

241. 1930 U.S. Census, Population Schedule, Ritters Twp., Moore Cty., North Carolina, E.D. 9, Sheet 14 B, Lines 84–91, www.ancestry.com (April 23, 2007). Bonnie Kay Donahue, "Farewell to a Friend: Bankruptcy Bar Remembers Judge Rufus Reynolds," *Disclosure Statement* (A Publication of the North Carolina Bar Association's Bankruptcy Section), Vol. 20, No. 2 (April 1999): 7, http://bankruptcy.ncbar.org/Newsletters/Bankruptcy+Newsletter+Archive/Downloads_GetFile.aspx?id=4399. (August 1, 2007). On Bernice Auman, see "Mr. Bernice Auman And Miss Reynolds United In Marriage," *The Courier* (June 6, 1929): 5.

242 Martha Johnson, daughter of Ivey and Ruby Luck, provided the biographical information about her father.

243 James Auman Bone (b.1945) provided the biographical information on his parents, James and Mildred Bone.

Index

exercises, commencement. *See* commencement; graduation

Eyes of Love (play), 24

F

Fairfield, AL, 82
Farlow, Amos, 51
Farlow, Elsie, 51
Farlow, Ruth, 51
Farm Life School, Moore County, NC, 3
farmers/farming, 1, **2**, 3, 8, 9, 11, 14, 15, 17, 18, 20, 22, 23, 35, 36, 39, 40, 42, 43, 45, 59, 70, 74, 75, 84, 95, 101, 111, 121, 122, 125, 162, 164
Fayetteville, NC, 25
Fayetteville Street School, Asheboro, NC, **33**
Fazenda, Louise (movie star), 124
Ferree, J.S. (or T.S.), 74, 157
Fiddlers' Conventions, 35
Fields, Charles Wesley, 38, 39
Fields, George, 148
Fields, Mae, 38, 39
Fields, Sarah Anne (née Auman) (Aunt Sarah), 38, **38**, 49
fights, 20
films. *See* movies (shows); silent films
First Division Pictures, 96
First National Pictures, 73, 78, 80
Fite, Craig, 65
Fite, Moyd Albridge, 65, 67, 68, 70, 148, 150
Flag Springs (church), 61
flappers, 110, 115
The Flat Tire (Scarberry), 100
Flennikan, Lena (née Russell), 165
flowers, 88, 89, 93, 94, 99, 138, 146

flu, 73, 74, 82
The Flying Fleet (movie), 91
Foch, General, 157
Fogleman, J. Archie, 146
food, 30, 31, 34, 36, 38, 42, 45, 47, 58, 68, 75, 82, 95, 98, 100, 101, 118, 119, 121, 123, 129, 132, 152, 154. *See also* candy
football
    games, 59, 64, 65, 67, 68, 71, 96, 120, 121, 122, 124
    players, 64, 140, 146
    teams, 139
Ford (car), 33, 42, 54, 57, 100, 127, 130
forensic contests, 93
Forest City, NC, 103
Forest Hills, NC, 86
Forsyth County, NC, 25
Fort Bragg, NC, 37
Fort Eustis, VA, 3
Fort Monroe, VA, 112
Fortress Monroe, VA, 60
fortunetelling, 94
Foss, Sam Walter, 97
Founce, Ruth, 50, 51, 54, 55
Four Million (O'Henry), 12
four-leaf clovers, 94
Fourth of July Parade (Asheboro, NC, 1920), **104**, 105
Fox Film Corporation, 85, 118, 123, 125, 134, 141
Fox Movietone Follies of 1929 (movie), 118
Francis, Alec, 73
Franklinville, NC, 6, 69
fraternities, 83, 139, 141
Frazier, Anna Grace, 9
Frazier, Rudolph, 9
French, Dorothy, 50, 54
Fuquay Springs, NC, 41

hospitals/hospital visits, 31, 36, 40, 41, 60, 142, 143

Hough, Louise (Louise Huff; Louise Huft), 56, 62, 65, 74, 76, 97, 121, 159

houses
  Alpheus Auman, **112**
  Belle and Dave Cornelison, **72**, 165
  Charlie T. Luck, **48**
  Claude Auman, **44**
  Frank Auman, **1**, **46**, 124, 142, 159, 161, **162**
  Howard Auman, 162, **164**
  Ivey Luck, **77**, 124
  Lebbeus Auman, **60**, 164

"The House by the Side of the Road" (Foss), 97

How to Study, 45

Howsare, Dr., 80, 82

Hoyle, Margaret Winfred, 102

Hudson, Mattie, 157

Hughes, Billy, 11

Hughes, Edwin, 158

Hughes, Mamie (née Luck) (Aunt Mamie), 11, 23, 47, 48

Hulm, Theodore, 45

Hulon, Theodore, 45

Hunter, Mary T. (college matron), 144, 146, 150

hunting, 75, 128, 130

Hyams, Leila, 117

I

illness. *See also* appendicitis; liver disease; measles; mumps; pneumonia; rheumatism; sickness
  flu at Seagrove, 73
  flu in North Carolina, 74
  Louie Zeigler, 82

Mary Elizabeth Auman, 162

Pete Williams, 78

Illusions (movie), 126

"I'm a Dreamer" (song), 141

initiation, 62

injuries
  Mary Elizabeth Auman, 98
  Thurman Cox, 125
  from wartime, 40

Iota Tau Kappa, 83, 139, 141

Irby, Dolphine Aleathea, 98

J

Jackson Springs, NC, 39, 40, 41, 43, 49, 50, 104

Jacob's Ladder, 15

Jacquet, Gaston (movie star), 126

James River Bridge, 112

The J.B. Cole Pottery, 28

Jessel, George (movie star), 134

Johnson, Margaret Sue, 88

Johnson, Martha, 185

Johnson, Mildred, 83, 116

Johnson, Mrs. C.C. (librarian), 83, 94

Johnson, O.W. (professor), 65

Johnson, Reverend J. Fuller, 41, 42

Jolson, Al (movie star), 66

Jones, Dace W., 84

Jones, Mary Rawles, 67, 157

Jozwiak, Katherine, 162

K

Keener, Suzanne (singer), 61

Keith, Curvie, 157

Kelly, George D., 94, 139

Kelly, George Edward, 70

Kelvinator, 100

Keyser, Ella Marie, 98, 99

killings, 124